THE ANCIENT VISITORS

THE ANCIENT
VISITORS

DANIEL COHEN

DOUBLEDAY & COMPANY, INC., GARDEN CITY, NEW YORK

to Dick Dempewolff

ISBN 0-385-09785-9 Trade
0-385-09786-7 Prebound
Library of Congress Catalog Card Number 75–21220

9 8 7 6 5

CONTENTS

THE ANCIENT VISITORS

1

THE ANCIENT VISITORS

Was the earth visited in ancient times by intelligent creatures from space?

Did these creatures transmit to us the knowledge that raised us above all the other animals on this planet?

Did they perhaps even artificially "create" the human race?

Are confused memories of these ancient visitors embedded in the religions and myths of all nations—in short, are the gods really intelligent extraterrestrials?

Can we find material evidence of these visits in the enormous monuments and startling technology of the ancients?

Are these extraterrestrials still with us today, guiding, in some unknown way, the development of the human race?

This is a startling series of questions, without doubt. But they are not nearly so startling today as they would have been a dozen or so years ago. Theories which answer a resounding yes to every one of these questions have become increasingly popular in recent years. But the theory of visits and control by extraterrestrial intelligences (or ETIs as I shall call them for the sake of brevity) have been around for quite a while.

The theme of visitors from space has been one of the staples of science fiction for many years. But we are not concerned in this book with acknowledged fiction. We are concerned with science. It is unorthodox science, to be sure, even bizarre science or possibly wrongheaded and crankish science—but science.

Where did the idea begin?

Charles Fort once wrote, "One measures a circle beginning anywhere." It has become sort of a motto for his followers. So let us begin with Charles Fort. He makes a good starting point for such a subject. Fort is not as famous as he should be, but to the real aficionados, he is the high priest of unorthodox, bizarre, wrongheaded, and crankish science.

Charles Hoy Fort was an American writer born in Albany, New York, August 9, 1874, died in the Bronx, May 3, 1932. In his younger years Fort traveled a good deal as a sort of itinerant journalist. He spent some time in London. But mostly he was in the Bronx. His fame, such as it is, rests primarily on the fact that he spent years collecting odd facts—facts that seemed to run counter to established scientific thinking of his time.

Fort disliked conventional astronomers and geologists and absolutely detested the evolutionary ideas of Charles Darwin. His mission (though he would have denied having any mission) was to knock the halo off science, to destroy what he thought had become the arrogant priesthood of science. His method was not a frontal attack, but guerrilla warfare—picking away at scientific theories with all sorts of things that seemed to contradict the established theories.

Fort wasn't very successful. His four books, *The Book of the Damned, New Lands, Lo!* and *Wild Talents*, were never really popular. Science continued despite him, and Fort was forgotten by all but a small and devoted band of followers. Today the name Fortean is

Charles Fort.

sometimes used to describe a person who collects odd facts. Yet Fort was one of the first, if not the first, to seriously propose the theory of extraterrestrial visitors that has become so popular today.

In addition to his four published works Fort wrote a couple of unpublished manuscripts called X and Y. Both were destroyed, but we have some idea of what they contained. According to Fort's biographer, Damon Knight:

"X was organized around the notion that our civilization is invisibly controlled by beings on the planet Mars . . . In Y, Fort imagined another sinister civilization a little closer at hand—at the South Pole. He considered that Kaspar Hauser, the mysterious boy who appeared in Nuremberg in 1828, was an emissary for 'Y-land' and that he was murdered to prevent his revealing the truth."

While Fort never attempted to have these particular ideas published, he later committed a very similar idea to print:

"I think we are property.

"I say we belong to something. That once upon a time this earth was a no-man's land, that other worlds explored and colonized here, and fought among themselves for possession, but now it's owned by something. And that something owns this earth and all others [have been] warned off."

Was Fort really serious? Was he really sane? All evidence indicates he was perfectly sane. However, we cannot be sure how serious he was. Fort liked to pose as the perfect skeptic. He professed to believe in nothing, not even his own theories. He liked to think of himself primarily as a humorist. But I suspect that humor was just a screen he tried to hide behind. I think he was perfectly serious when he wrote, "I think we are property."

Fort died before the space program was ever dreamed of. He was gone twenty years before UFOs became an obsession with a lot of people. He wrote before scientists made any real attempt to contact intelligences in outer space. He was ahead of his time— not necessarily correct, mind you, merely premature.

When the possibility that we could contact other planets became a reality, it was almost natural to turn the situation around and wonder if perhaps other planets were not trying to contact us—to even wonder if they already had.

A lot of people speculated, either tentatively or enthusiastically, on the possibility. The unlikely figure who reaped the reward of all this speculation was a Swiss hotel man named Erich von Däniken. His book *Chariots of the Gods?*, published in 1969, stated flatly that there was solid evidence that ETIs had visited our planet thousands of years ago. Von Däniken used this idea to explain a lot of unexplained things about the world. *Chariots of the Gods?* was a fantastic success. It has sold millions of copies and been translated into a score of languages. It was the basis for a popular movie and two highly successful TV specials. It has made Erich von Däniken a rich man.

The book so established Von Däniken that his reputation as prophet of a whole new view of human history was unshaken by the wide publicity given to the fact that he was jailed in Switzerland for fraud. The case against him had nothing whatever to do with his theories, but during the trial a court psychiatrist who had examined Von Däniken described him as a prestige-seeker, a liar, and an unstable and criminal psychopath with a hysterical character.

Accurate or not, that sort of a denunciation, and a conviction for fraud, embezzlement, and forgery is likely to shake anybody's reputation, particularly if that person happens to be proposing wildly unorthodox theories. An unstained reputation for truth telling is normally very useful to people who intend to show that all the experts are wrong.

Von Däniken spent his year in jail composing his second book *The Gods from Outer Space.* It was very nearly as successful as his first. And if, as they say, imitation is the sincerest form of flattery, Erich von Däniken has been mightily flattered by a flood of imitations.

Erich von Däniken.

And yet Von Däniken's books contain little that is really new. The "mysteries" and "enigmas" that he discusses had been repeatedly examined and pondered over by other writers. His solution of visitors from space is also not new. As we have seen, it is at least as old as Charles Fort. Von Däniken, however, is more of an optimist. He sees the ETIs as benevolent bringers of civilization, rather than as mysterious and sinister "owners."

But the theories of ETI visitation are not limited to Von Däniken and Fort. It has become one of those subjects upon which practically everyone seems to have done some speculating.

The subject is a hard one to define in conventional terms. It gets into astronomy, physics, biology, archaeology, history, anthropology, psychology, theology, and continues on to the nether regions of mysticism and occultism. Like a giant amoeba it seems to have no boundaries, and no particular shape. More distressing yet, like an amoeba, it seems to absorb every bit of information in its path. Practically everything from antigravity machines to the size of the human brain, has been turned into grist for the ETI theorists' mill.

One can hardly hope to present all the evidence on this subject. What I hope to do here is present a representative sample of evidence, from as many sources as possible.

I hesitate to say that the presentation will be objective. I am no longer sure that word has a very useful meaning. In practice an objective writer is generally one with whom the reader already agrees. Most of us are so very sure what we believe is correct that it does not seem possible that anyone who thinks differently could possibly be objective.

This is a controversial subject. The person who does not have some kind of an opinion on a controversial subject either doesn't know about it or doesn't care. Often writers will present a lot of material that they know is nonsense under the guise of "being objective."

Even when a writer does not try to beat his readers over the head with a particular point of view, opinions tend to come through. They dictate the choice of evidence, and the very choice of words. The best I can hope to do is try to present a balanced view of the arguments for and against the theory of ETI visitation. I'm not going to try to build a case for either side.

Naturally, though, I have opinions about the evidence. These will be revealed in the final chapter, though I suspect most readers will have guessed what they are long before that. If you are impatient you can jump ahead and read the final chapter now. I don't recommend that. I think that books should be read in the ordinary way from front to back. But this isn't a whodunit. The book will not be spoiled if you read the "solution" first. That is because there really is no solution, just an opinion. And my opinion may not necessarily be any better than anyone else's. You may arrive at quite a different set of conclusions.

The fun of the book is in the evidence. I would like to stress the idea of fun, because this isn't a very practical sort of book. This book isn't going to help you repair cars, or do embroidery, or cook. It isn't even going to help you pass any tests, for as far as I know there are no recognized courses on ancient astronauts— at least not yet—though that may be coming.

If this book is to have any practical use at all it is to provide a little exercise for the mind, some stretching that will help to tone up an imagination grown a bit flabby in our humdrum everyday world. For a while we can let the dreary business of simply getting through the day be forgotten. We are going to be dealing with the really big questions, about the universe, the origin of life, and the meaning of it all.

So let's get on with it.

The Earth as seen from space. NASA

2

IS ANYONE OUT THERE?

Speculating about the possibilities of life in outer space, particularly intelligent life, is taking a long leap into the dark. But before we can really approach the question of whether or not intelligent extraterrestrials ever visited the earth, we have to at least make a stab at answering the question of whether there are intelligent extraterrestrials in the first place.

Let us start very simply. Our sun is a star. It is orbited by nine planets, one of which contains intelligent life. We can be quite sure of this because the intelligent life is us. Beyond this basic certainty, however, lie a multitude of uncertainties. We will ignore all those jokes that ask, "Is there intelligent life on earth?"

The next question is, do any of the other planets in this solar system contain intelligent life? The best guess is probably not. Intelligent and highly advanced Martians, and Venusians and Saturnians have, of course, appeared regularly in science fiction—but most scientists, even those ready to engage in unbuttoned speculation about extraterrestrial life, have not been enthusiastic about the prospect of intelligent life on other planets in our solar system for many years now.

About a century ago, the Italian astronomer Giovanni Schiaparelli discovered what he thought was an intricate network of straight lines on the planet Mars. He called these lines *canali,* which means "channels." However, the Italian word was mistranslated into the English word "canals." The suspicious straightness of the lines combined with the mistranslation led to a flowering of speculation about the intelligent Martians who had built this network of canals in order to irrigate their dry planet.

A lot of astronomers simply couldn't see Schiaparelli's *canali,* and they suspected that his astonishing sighting was really an optical illusion. But the controversy was taken up by the great American astronomer Percival Lowell. Lowell not only saw canals, he saw oases which appeared to grow and shrink according to the season, thus marking the ebb and flow of Martian agriculture. Lowell came to be regarded as the patron saint of the Intelligent Life on Mars School.

A French astronomer and popularizer of science, Camille Flammarion, went Lowell and Schiaparelli one better—he thought he detected vegetation growing on the moon.

Even before the moon landings it had been generally accepted among scientists that there was no life on the moon. The Martian canal controversy also died down long ago, for when telescopic observation of Mars became more accurate, the "canals" failed to show themselves. Photographs sent back by Mars probes have confirmed that there is no extensive network of canals on Mars.

The moons of Mars provide us with several puzzles. Mars's two small moons, named Deimos and Phobos,

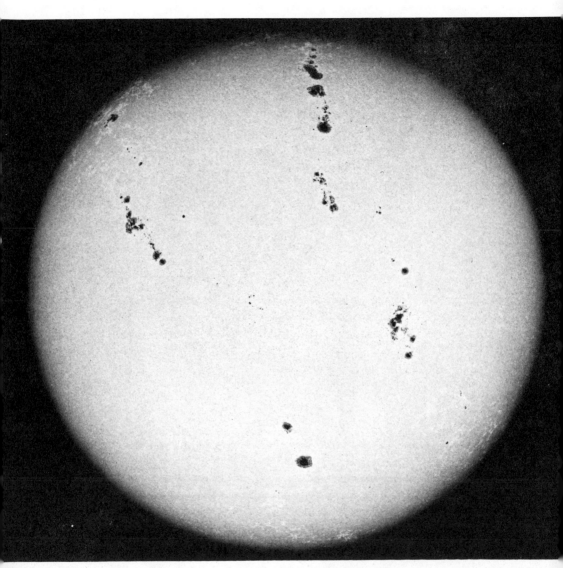

The Sun.   MOUNT WILSON AND PALOMAR

Mars photographed by the Mariner 9 space probe. NASA

were not actually observed until 1877. But their presence had been predicted over 150 years earlier by the English satirist Jonathan Swift in the book now called *Gulliver's Travels*. Not only did Swift predict that Mars had two satellites, but he described their size and orbital period with a passable degree of accuracy.

This incident has been regarded as an outstanding example of a lucky accident. For there is no indication that Swift was actually trying to predict anything. In *Gulliver's Travels*, Swift has a lot of wild things to say about distant lands or other planets. None of these things, aside from the statements about the moons of Mars, has turned out to be accurate. Fire enough shots, marksmen agree, and you are bound to hit something.

But ETI theorists do not take Swift's statements so lightly. They hint that Jonathan Swift may have had access to some secret astronomical knowledge, handed down by a supercivilization of the past and only redis-covered in 1877.

There are also some peculiar things about the moons of Mars. They are only ten and five miles in diameter. Yet they are far brighter than they should be. Their orbits are nearly circular, and they pass almost directly over the planet's equator. There are other more tech-nical peculiarities about their orbits as well. All of which make Deimos and Phobos seem more like the artificial satellites than natural satellites. Maybe they are artificial satellites, suggested I. S. Shklovsky, a dis-tinguished and outspoken Soviet astronomer. Maybe they are made of polished metal, and that is why they are so bright, he added. Shklovsky admitted that the idea was a fantastic one, but asked if anyone had any better suggestions to explain the peculiarities of the two satellites.

The Soviet astronomer theorized that the satellites might have been put up by some extinct Martian civilization. But the American scientist Frank Salisbury had a more startling idea—they were artificial all right, but of comparatively recent origin. Salisbury noted that conditions for viewing Mars had been better in 1862 than in 1877, when the satellites were actually discovered. And in 1862 the scientists were using a larger telescope to observe Mars. Why couldn't they find Deimos and Phobos then? Perhaps because they weren't there, but had been put up between 1862 and 1877, Salisbury suggested.

These are admittedly speculations, and scientifically they are wild ones with little support in the scientific community.

But the question of life on Mars is not really settled. Information received from various probes of Mars indicate that conditions on the planet may support life. There is, for example, evidence of more water than had previously been suspected. There is no active expectation among astronomers that Mars contains any high civilizations, or in fact any kind of intelligent life. But there is a hope that it might contain microscopic life of some sort. A variety of scientific instruments designed to test this theory will be landed on Mars in the middle of 1976.

There is less hope of finding any form of life on other planets in our solar system—they are too hot or too cold or have atmospheres composed of noxious gases. But even the discovery of microbes on Mars would make a significant contribution to the case for intelligent life in outer space. It would indicate that the conditions under which life can begin are not unique

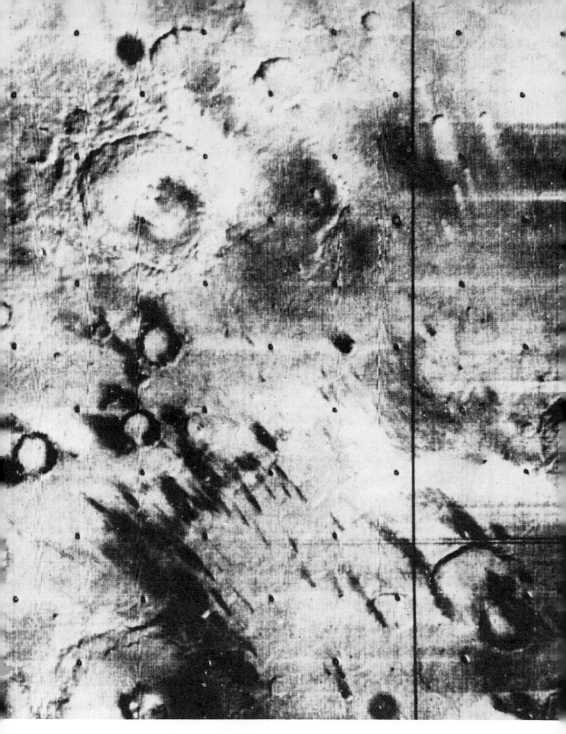

The surface of Mars as photographed by Mariner 9. NASA

to this planet. It would mean that at the least two planets out of nine in our solar system contain life, and one of them, Earth, contains intelligent life.

The hope of finding intelligent life somewhere in the universe rests not so much on the planets of our own solar system, but on planets circling other stars, and there are an awful lot of stars.

Most of us live in cities where the night sky is obscured by smog and city lights. We tend to forget how many stars there are. But sometimes in the country, on a clear night, we can look up into the sky and almost be staggered by the number of stars we see. How many stars are there? I suppose practically everyone has spent a fruitless hour or two trying to count the stars in the sky. I never got much beyond fifty, because I would lose my place and not remember whether I had counted a particular group of stars before or not. Astronomers estimate that somewhere around four thousand stars are visible to the naked eye. But that is just the beginning, for we can only detect the brightest or closest of these stars. With telescopes astronomers are able to identify somewhere in the neighborhood of two million stars—and that may be just a beginning.

Our sun is located on the edge of a spiral-shaped galaxy or cluster of stars we call the Milky Way. This galaxy contains billions of stars, perhaps as many as two hundred billion—we don't know for sure, because there are large portions of our galaxy which we cannot see. And even that is only the beginning, for we know that there are many more star-rich galaxies in the universe—no one knows how many for no one knows the size of the universe—or if indeed the universe has any limits at all. When we begin to speculate on subjects

The Moon.   LICK OBSERVATORY

such as the number of stars in the universe we are dealing with numbers that are too large to comprehend, and too large to have any real meaning. It is sufficient to say that there are an enormous number of stars.

Life doesn't start on stars—though the possibility has been speculated upon—it starts on planets. How many of the stars in the universe have planets circling them?

Gulliver III, one of the devices designed to detect living microorganisms on Mars. After landing, small projectiles with sticky strings attached are fired a short distance away. The strings are reeled back, and any living material stuck to them can be detected. This information will be radioed back to earth. NASA

A general consensus among astronomers is that solar systems like our own are fairly common. But since there is no general agreement among astronomers about how our own solar system started, it is difficult for them to estimate how many similar systems may have been formed elsewhere. Astronomers believe that they have direct evidence of a planetary system circling a nearby star. We have no direct evidence at all about any of the other stars, but scientists assume that our solar system is not unique, therefore there must also be an enormous number of other planetary systems circling other stars.

Next we come up against the problem of how many of these planets would be capable of supporting life. At this point purists often raise the question "What is life?" and go on to speculate about "life forms" that can live on the surface of stars, or in the absolute zero of interstellar space. We have enough problems already, so we will limit our inquiry to "life as we know it"— that is life which displays the same basic properties as life here on earth. For such life we need planets that are neither too hot nor too cold, large enough to hold an atmosphere, and small enough to allow the development of free oxygen, and an earth-type atmosphere.

In estimating the number of possibly habitable planets in the universe astronomers can be roughly divided into two groups, optimists and pessimists. The optimists set the number of habitable planets in the billions, the pessimists set the number in the millions. Both are very large numbers by earthly standards.

How many of the possibly habitable planets really are inhabited? Over the last few years astronomers have found evidence that the chemical compounds

Star clouds in the Milky Way.   MOUNT WILSON AND PALOMAR

which form the basis of life are fairly common throughout the universe. This raises the probability that life has begun on other planets but does not make it a certainty, because we don't know how life began in the first place. We have some good theories, but at present that is all they are.

Next question—if life did develop would it inevitably evolve toward intelligence? Next answer—who knows? Again we must be guided by the general principle which holds that earthly conditions are not unique in the universe, and that some sort of an intelligence would evolve elsewhere, though it might be quite alien to us.

We have piled one supposition on top of another, and it may appear that the result is a rather rickety pile of guesswork. Well, perhaps that is so. But we start out with one hard fact—the enormous number of stars in the universe—and one pretty hard guess—a large number of planets capable of supporting life. A general consensus among astronomers would hold that some form of life must exist on millions or billions of other planets, and on at least some of these there must be intelligent life.

The prevailing view about life in the universe was stated very elegantly by science writer Walter Sullivan in his popular and influential book *We Are Not Alone:*

"The universe that lies about us, visible only in the privacy, the intimacy of night, is incomprehensibly vast. Yet the conclusion that life exists across this vastness seems inescapable. We cannot yet be sure whether or not it lies within reach, but in any case, we are part of it all; we are not alone!"

Sullivan touches upon the second part of the life in space problem—can we reach it, or, more to the point in this case, can it reach us? The sheer vastness of space presents an enormous problem. Stars are so far away from us that distances must be measured in light years—that is the distance that light can travel in a year. Light travels at a speed of 186,000 miles a second. The closest star is 4.3 light years away. It is a distance that beggars earthly comparison—and that is only the closest star. While intelligent life may indeed exist on the universe we have no particular reason to believe that it exists on any "nearby" star.

Enthusiasts for extraterrestrial visitation sometimes treat the problem of distance a bit cavalierly. After all, they say, it took Ferdinand Magellan's crew three years to complete their circumnavigation of the globe. So extraterrestrial explorers from a nearby star, a ship traveling at the speed of light might need only four or five earthly years to make the trip from their star to ours. And these extraterrestrials might have far longer life spans than human beings.

We can concede the possibility, even the probability, of longer life spans, but it is not so easy to concede the possibility of a craft that travels at the speed of light or anything near to it. Indeed there is a good deal of evidence that points to the conclusion that a craft traveling at or near the speed of light is simply impossible.

That, however, may be a narrow view, conditioned by the limitations of our earthly intelligence. Life has existed on this planet (according to current estimates) for about two billion years. Something roughly resembling a human being for about two million. In a

A spiral galaxy.   HALE OBSERVATORIES

few thousand years we have gone from the horse-drawn carriage to the moon rocket. There may be planets on which intelligent life has been evolving for millions or even billions of years. There may be life forms out there which have evolved a technology beyond anything we know or can possibly imagine.

The most ambitious earthly attempt to contact ETIs did not involve direct contact, but rather it was an attempt to pick up signals. The attempt was called Project Ozma. When it was launched in 1960 it attracted a good deal of publicity. It seemed to indicate that scientists were at last taking the possibility of extraterrestrial life seriously. Actually, they had been serious about the possibility for some time, but until 1960 there was nothing that they could really do.

In Project Ozma a giant radio-telescope was trained on two nearby stars. The aim was to pick up any pattern of signals that might be interpreted as being intelligently directed. There were a couple of false alarms, as the scientists picked up signals of earthly origin. Project director Dr. Frank Drake said these signals set off a "moderate amount of pandemonium" in the control room. But it was all a mistake. Over 150 hours of scanning produced nothing interesting, and the radio-telescope was turned to other projects. Scientists said, quite reasonably, that Project Ozma was only a trial run, and that they could hardly expect to pick up signals on the first try. But there is no doubt that those who worked on the project were disappointed.

A space probe launched in 1972 and due to leave our solar system contains a plaque bearing a picture of a man and woman and a number of signs and symbols that scientists think might make sense to an intelligent extraterrestrial.

This is very much the note-in-the-bottle approach to searching for other intelligences. We are shooting a probe off into the vastness of space with a message, in the hopes that somebody out there might find it. That is what a castaway on a desert island does when he puts a note in a bottle and tosses it into the sea. He hopes it will be washed up on a distant shore and be found by someone who can read it. But the sea into which we are casting our space bottle is incomparably vaster than any earthly ocean. There is not a great deal of hope that it is going to result in anything. But what is the harm in trying?

Our attempts to contact intelligences in space have been almost pitifully inadequate. But in this case man may not be the measure of all things.

So one cannot dismiss out of hand the possibility that extraterrestrials have not only developed craft that can travel at or near the speed of light, but beyond the speed of light.

One of the best-established scientific principles is that the speed of light is the absolute speed in the universe —nothing goes faster. And yet, recently a distinguished physicist advanced an idea that there might be particles that he called taceyons that travel faster than the speed of light. The speed of light may not be absolute. Or what about craft that cut across the curvature of space (if indeed there is such a thing) or through time itself?

It is also possible that extraterrestrials might be willing to undertake voyages lasting hundreds or thousands of years. They might live hundreds or thousands of years, or they might spend most of the voyage in a state of suspended animation, or generations of them might be committed to completing the voyage.

27

Another problem—why would extraterrestrials want to come to this planet in the first place? We have already postulated the possible existence of millions or billions of habitable planets. What makes us so interesting that ETIs would be willing to embark upon voyages of incredible length to reach us? And upon reaching us, why have they not made their presence known in a more direct and forceful manner?

Theories vary—but the general opinion among those who believe in extraterrestrial contact is that the first contact took place thousands of years ago and had a profound influence on the human race. There have been repeated contacts since that time, but they are reported to us by our ancestors as contacts with gods or spirits. Many believe that the ETIs are still hovering about earth in their spaceships, which we call UFOs.

In the opinion of some there exists a vast intergalactic civilization with a mission to spread its knowledge from solar system to solar system. The ETIs deliberately pick out inhabited planets and help guide the most intelligent creatures on the planet toward a level of development where they too will be able to become conscious and contributing members of this intergalactic web. The reason the ETIs have been so coy about fully revealing themselves and their purposes is that they do not wish the human race to suffer the culture shock of being confronted with a vastly superior species.

Such knowledge thrust suddenly upon us might plunge us into confusion and despair, particularly if it were also known that many of our proudest accomplishments were not ours alone but were in fact directed by the ETIs. Thus, the theory goes, the ETIs have preferred to hide behind myth, legend, and mystery, awaiting the day when we are "ready" for "the Truth."

The human race is certainly more willing to accept the possibility of extraterrestrial contact now than it was, say, half a century ago. The space program, scientific speculation about extraterrestrial life, thirty years of UFO sightings, and an awful lot of science fiction have in a sense prepared us for the possibility. We might well be shocked and depressed by the firm knowledge that we are not the most intelligent creatures around, but we would not be entirely surprised.

Many are really quite enthusiastic about the prospect. Max H. Flindt and Otto O. Binder end their book *Mankind—Child of the Stars* with this glowing vision:

"We seem exposed today to a vast unknown that Man's mind has not yet encompassed. We are perhaps on the verge of the greatest revelations known in history. We may learn, soon perhaps, that we are only one tiny part of a Grand Family of humans stretching to the remotest star.

"If so, it should be met with revel and joy to know that we are citizens not of one world, but of the great and wondrous universe."

Not all of those who believe that we have been and still are being visited by ETIs are quite so optimistic. Some even suspect dark and evil purposes behind such visits. Charles Fort spoke of our planet being "owned." But in general, ETI theorists are more optimistic about motives and capabilities of the extraterrestrials, than they are about the motives and capabilities of the human race.

Any discussion of extraterrestrial intelligence is by its very nature a highly speculative enterprise. But discussing the possible motivation of an alien race, whose thought processes everyone admits may be entirely incomprehensible to us, really seems to pass the boundary of legitimate speculation. It is fun, of course, but we cannot hope to arrive at any sort of conclusion at all.

Since we are not going to get anywhere trying to decide whether ETIs could or would visit us—we must bring the problem back to earth and try to see if there is any evidence that they have visited us. That is what we will do in the following chapters.

3

MONUMENTS TO SPACE?

Of all the evidence mustered to support the theory of extraterrestrial intervention in human affairs, the gigantic lines and figures of the Nazca Desert in Peru are probably the most interesting. Unlike the pyramids of Egypt, the statues of Easter Island and other monuments which involve moving great weights, there is no particular puzzle as to how the lines and figures were made—the puzzle is by whom and for what purpose?

Very few people had ever even heard of the figures in the Nazca before the late 1950s, though they had been seen many times. The region in which these figures are located is extremely inhospitable. "Hot enough to boil your brains," one traveler complained. Still people did pass through it, and they probably noticed strange and obviously artificial "lines" etched in the desert surface. But the lines didn't mean too much from ground level. As planes began to pass over the Nazca region they began to notice that some of these lines were really parts of huge figures, whose shape could only be appreciated from an airplane. Aerial photographs of the region proved to be highly dramatic.

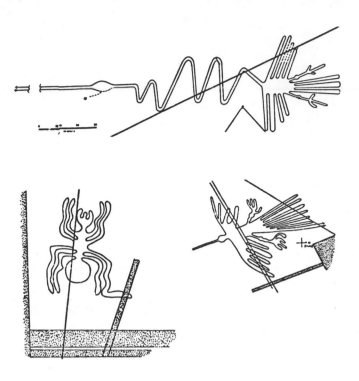

Some of the figures of the Nazca Desert.

Therein lies the basic mystery and allure of the Nazca figures—why would anyone bother to make figures that could only be appreciated from an airplane in an era when there were no airplanes? For it is well established that these drawings are at least fifteen hundred years old.

The Nazca is not the only site of colossal figures. Above the Bay of Piaco in Peru, there is incised into the surface what looks like a huge, three-branched candlestick. Large figures of one sort or another are found throughout the American Southwest. Nor are such colossal figures limited to the New World. Figures of what look like giants or huge horses are found on limestone cliffs in various parts of the British Isles.

Most of these figures can be appreciated from a distance, for they are on hillsides. One gets quite a good view of the "candlestick" from the Bay of Piaco. What makes the figures of the Nazca really special is that they are on a plateau and that there is absolutely no way of appreciating them from the surface.

There is a variety of figures—birds, spiders, fishes, even a monkey, and a couple of unidentifiable creatures. There are also rectangular shapes, and a variety of straight lines or "roads" which run, apparently, from nowhere to nowhere. The surface in which the figures and lines are incised is made up of gravel and pebbles. It is often called desert pavement. To form the lines, the rocks and pebbles have been moved to expose the lighter soil beneath. The rocks are then piled up on each side of the line. From the air the figures and lines might seem etched by a light-colored line, which is itself outlined by two darker filaments. When the sun is low, the little piles of pebbles cast long shadows which make the outlines of the drawings clearer.

How could such fragile drawings have survived for hundreds of years? The secret lies not in any technical marvels within the drawings themselves but in the distinctive weather of the area in which they are located. The Nazca Desert is on a high plateau about sixty miles long and five miles wide. It is on the coast of Peru, some 250 miles south of the capital of Lima. A cold ocean current cuts through the warmer waters of the southern Pacific and brushes the coast. Moist ocean air passing over this cold water is effectively blocked from dumping its moisture until it is pushed up over the Andes Mountains, which rise steeply from the western edge of the desert. Half of the year the sky is clear and the surface of the desert is blazingly hot. For much of the other half of the year fog shrouds the desert, but still no rain falls.

In this virtually rainless land there is minimal erosion. The lines in the desert will not fade for centuries, even millennia, if undisturbed by man. The only change is that the lighter lines gradually darken as a result of the chemical action of the air on the exposed rocks.

We don't know how the drawings were actually made, since their creators could never get a good view of the finished product. But it is generally assumed that they first made a scale model of the drawing, and then marked out the large drawing on the desert, using calibrated ropes for measurement. The straight lines were apparently laid out using logs as sighting posts. One of these logs was still in place, and through the use of radiocarbon dating scientists were able to determine it came from a tree cut down fifteen hundred years ago. That is the only reliable date we have for the Nazca figures.

Who made these figures? Again no certain answer can be given. The first guess was that they were made by the Incas, for the Incas who had once controlled the region were monumental builders. At one time the straight lines were rather casually referred to as Inca roads. But that cannot be, for the lines are clearly not roads. A real Inca road does run through the figures, partially obliterating some of them. Apparently the Incas didn't care much about the figures, if they were even aware of them. Besides the Inca empire did not exist fifteen hundred years ago.

The land, of course, was not uninhabited before the coming of the Incas. A people we call the Nazcas, had been able, by careful cultivation, to farm some of the western parts of the desert, using water runoff from the mountains. Racially and culturally the Nazcas were quite close to the Incas, who were themselves basically a single tribe or group that had been able to establish a military superiority over similar people who inhabited a wide area. The Nazcas had no written language, nor did the Incas who conquered them. If there were any Nazcas left who had any knowledge of the figures they were wiped out after the Spanish conquest of the Inca empire, so that piece of history is quite blank. All we can say for certain is that some of the figures match designs found on Nazca pottery.

While the figures present no really difficult technical problems, they still must have taken a long time to construct. The Nazcas, like most technologically primitive peoples, probably did not have much time to spare from the hard business of getting enough food to eat. So to divert a lot of labor into making these figures indicates that the figures meant a great deal to them. But what did they mean? That, is where speculation takes off.

First of all, we can rule out the road idea with certainty. An interesting explanation was advanced by an American scholar, Paul Koosk, who was first responsible for bringing the lines and figures to public attention. Koosk said that they represented "the largest astronomy book in the world." He got this idea almost as a revelation. He and his wife visited Peru in 1941. On June 22, the winter solstice, hence the shortest day of the year in the Southern Hemisphere, they were standing in the Nazca Desert, pondering the possible significance of the lines, as the sun began to set. They saw that the setting sun touched the horizon right over one of the lines at whose base they stood.

Koosk died before he could expand much on his theory, but the work was taken up by Dr. Maria Reiche, a German-born astronomer and mathematician. Dr. Reiche became a passionate apostle of the Nazca figures. She almost singlehandedly held off land developers who threatened to destroy a major portion of the area. She has also measured and photographed the lines and figures with fanatical intensity. From her researches Dr. Reiche has worked out a large number of astronomical correlations. She has shown, for example, how certain "fixed" stars rose and set over the lines, and thus could have been used by the astronomer-priests of the Nazcas for their own computations.

But Dr. Reiche's conclusions have not been accepted by other scientists. The basic problem is that there are a lot of lines, and a lot of possible astronomical correlations. The relationship between the rising of stars or the setting of the sun at different times of year with some of the lines may have been deliberate. But some given the huge number of possibilities, these relationships might also be accidental. The evidence is not overwhelming either way.

One major stumbling block in the way of scientific respectability for Dr. Reiche's theories is that if all of her astronomical calculations are correct they imply that the Nazcas had far greater astronomical knowledge than previously imagined. The South American Indians were exceptionally good astronomers, but most scientists doubt they were that good. Unless, of course, they got help from somewhere.

Now we come to the most sensational explanation of

all. It was stated bluntly by Von Däniken in *Chariots of the Gods?* "Seen from the air, the clear-cut impression that the 37-mile-long plain of Nazca made on *me* was that of an airfield."

This startling idea did not originate with Von Däniken. In *Flights into Yesterday,* a book on aerial archaeology, Professor Leo Deuel notes, "For a number of years the Nazca 'sand drawings,' though by then a fairly familiar landmark, were looked upon as little but an odd curiosity. Facetiously they were dubbed 'prehistoric landing fields,' or invited comparisons with the canals of Mars. Indeed, a Martian aura clung to them for quite a while." It still clings to them.

In the mid-1960s, long before the Von Däniken book became popular, UFO lecturers were showing slides of the Nazca, and proclaiming it as a landing field for UFOs in ancient times.

Let us accept this line of speculation for the moment. Would spaceships piloted by ETIs have really needed elaborately marked landing fields? Since UFO landings have been reported in unmarked fields, and even in the sea, it seems unlikely that they would need runways more suitable, perhaps, for jumbo jets.

If not landing fields then, perhaps messages for the gods. Since the figures could only be truly appreciated from the air, it is reasonable to assume that they were meant for gods that lived in or came from the sky. Here we find orthodox scientists and ETI speculators in rare agreement. In both views the figures were meant as messages for sky gods. The disagreement comes over the nature of these gods—were they mythical or extraterrestrial?

While speculation over the Nazca figures is compara-

The Great Sphinx and the Great Pyramid.

tively recent, speculation on the how and why of the Great Pyramid is well over a century old. There are actually many pyramids in Egypt, but the largest of them the Great Pyramid at Giza is the one that excites the most attention. The pyramids of Egypt never really had to be discovered. They have been tourist attractions for centuries. The earliest written records that we have of them come from the Greek traveler Herodotus who saw them in the fifth century B.C. They were ancient even then. Herodotus' guides told him that the pyramids had been built as tombs for the kings of Egypt in ancient times. That is the universally accepted scientific explanation for them today.

But there is no such unanimity as to how they were built. The most popular guess is that as the pyramid rose, a ramp was built, either up to it or corkscrewed around it. The huge blocks were then dragged up the ramp. Herodotus spoke of some sort of wooden lifting machine, and some students of ancient engineering believe that the builders employed a rather simple but effective sort of wooden derrick that could lift heavy stones from one tier to the next.

There is archaeological disagreement as to how the Egyptians could have dressed or finished the stones so that not even a knife blade could be slipped between them. There is even disagreement over how the stones were quarried and transported to the pyramid site. But there is no substantial doubt among serious archaeologists that it was possible for technologically primitive people, such as it is assumed the Egyptians were, to construct such monuments without resort to magic, or an unknown supertechnology. The main ingredients in constructing the pyramids, and indeed all ancient monuments, say the archaeologists, was the lavish expenditure of time and human muscle.

But there are doubters now as there have been for the last century and a half. Says one of the leading supporters of the ETI visitation theory: "Who nowadays can still accept the 'serious archaeological explanation' that these stone blocks were moved up inclined planes using wooden rollers? The sides of the stones are dressed so accurately that they were fitted together without mortar."

Aside from the sheer physical difficulties of constructing a monument like the Great Pyramid, it presents some difficulties in planning, as well. For example, to calculate the proper angle at which a pyramid should be constructed appears to take a fairly sophisticated knowledge of geometry, a knowledge which archaeologists are fairly certain that the ancient Egyptians did not possess. Were they then given some sort of secret knowledge? Many contended they were, but archaeologists have theorized a number of practical, though time-consuming methods the Egyptians could have used without the mathematical theory.

One of the more astonishing things about the Great Pyramid is that the sides of the base are oriented to within one tenth of a degree of the true north-south and east-west directions. The orientation is so nearly perfect that it could hardly have been an accident. But how could the Egyptians have determined true north, for, as far as we know, they possessed no compass? One explanation was suggested by the archaeological writer L. Sprague De Camp:

"A possible method is to build an artificial horizon—that is a circular wall, high enough so that a person seated in the center cannot see any earthly objects over the top of the wall. The seated observer, with his head at the center of the circle, watches a star rise (any bright northerly star would do) and directs another surveyor to mark the place on the wall where the star appeared. When that same star sets, he causes another mark to be made. By lowering a plumb bob from the marks on the wall, the surveyors find the places at the foot of the wall, inside, and directly below the marks. They then draw lines to the center of the circle. By bisecting the angle between these lines with cords and markings they determine the true north."

Such explanations, however logical they may be, do not carry much conviction to those outside of the scientific community, for they seem just too complex, for "simple" and "primitive" peoples to have carried out. It is far more reasonable to believe in secret knowledge passed down from some superior intelligence.

And yet, if the Egyptians had been given secret engineering knowledge, why didn't they use it on all of their pyramids? There is evidence that some pyramids collapsed before they were finished and the projects had to be abandoned. In other pyramids the orientation is not nearly so exact as in the Great Pyramid. Why not?

So far we have been speaking of the Great Pyramid as if it had been built by the ancient Egyptians. But there have been numerous objections raised to such an assumption. Some of these objections have been based on racial or religious grounds—that is a belief or prejudice that brown-skinned pagans could not possibly have had the brains to construct such a magnificent monument. The British occultist Basil Steward insisted in his book *The Mystery of the Great Pyramid* that it was designed and begun by a single individual "who belonged to the Adamic White civilization endowed with moral, scientific and cultural attainments far in advance of all other contemporary civilizations."

John Taylor, a nineteenth-century Englishman who became obsessed with the Great Pyramid, though he never laid eyes on it, decided that the builders of the pyramid were of "the chosen race in the line of, though preceding Abraham; so early indeed as to be closer to Noah than to Abraham." Some people misinterpreted Taylor, and believed he said that Noah himself had directed the building of the Great Pyramid. Well, why not, after overseeing the construction of the Ark, who would be better to direct the building of this other great project?

Those who hold grandiose theories about the origin of the Great Pyramid are not content with the notion that it was only a big tomb for an old Egyptian king, it must, they insist, be something more. What more might it be? Perhaps a repository for all manner of ancient wisdom. They did not regard the Great Pyramid as an ancient library; the "wisdom of the ages" was not stored in it—it was built in it. By interpretation of the various measurements of the Great Pyramid, some believed that one could do such things as calculate the distance from the earth to the sun, the circumference of the earth, the frequency of eclipses, and an enormous host of other geographical and astronomical information. A whole science, or pseudoscience, called pyramidology, sprang up.

And the pyramidologists went further. They said that by proper interpretation of measurements, the earth's past could be revealed; they could find the date of the Flood, when the Hebrews were expelled from Egypt, the time of Christ's birth, and so forth. Many of these events had occurred after the pyramid had been built, and thus it was assumed the pyramid could be used to predict the future. And there the pyramidologists ran into a lot of trouble. While they were excellent at relating the measurements of the pyramid to events that had taken place before the interpretation was being made, they were less reliable about events still in the future. They predicted the Second Coming of Christ and start of the Millennium so many times that pyramidology became something of a joke. Scholars referred to such individuals as pyramidiots.

While use of the Great Pyramid as an instrument of prophecy has declined considerably in recent years, there is still plenty of speculation about other "secrets in the pyramids." Most persistent is the contention that the builders of the Great Pyramid possessed all sorts of incredible astronomical and geographical and mathematical knowledge—knowledge far beyond what should have been available to the ancient Egyptians.

In a popular book called *Secrets of the Great Pyramid*, author Peter Tompkins concludes "Whatever mystical, occult or science-fiction tales may be associated with the Great Pyramid, it is still an extra-ordinary piece of masonry, and its designers must have been extra-ordinary beings. Who they were and when they built their Pyramid remains a mystery. So the quest continues. . . . But as more is discovered it may open the door to a whole new civilization of the past, and a much longer history of man than has heretofore been credited."

This is not the opinion of the professionals. They see all the marvelous numerical correlations in the Great Pyramid as the result of simply playing around with an enormous number of measurements, until one comes up with the inevitable correlations. However the pyramidologists' view fits perfectly with those who hold the ETIs imparted many lost secrets of science to an ancient civilization.

Next to the Great Pyramid, there has probably been

more speculation lavished on the builders and purposes of Stonehenge than on any other monument anywhere.

Practically everyone is familiar with what Stonehenge looks like. It is a circle of huge stones, the most impressive of them being the trilithons. These are sets of three stones, two uprights, weighing perhaps forty-five tons each, topped by a lintel. The total effect is rather like a narrow doorway. Though Stonehenge is partly fallen today, and many of its original stones are missing, it is still possible to get a pretty good idea of what it once looked like.

Though not on a scale with the Great Pyramid, Stonehenge is an impressive monument. We know that the largest of the stones were moved to their present location from over twenty miles away, and that some of

Stonehenge.

the stones were apparently brought from Wales a distance of some 130 miles. As usual there are those who claim that the stones could not have been moved great distances, or set up as they were, by normal human means. They invoke magic or unknown technology. But archaeologists are unanimous in their belief that no unknown forces were necessary. Again the "secret," if it can be called that, is the application of tremendous amounts of labor over a long period of time.

There is somewhat more genuine controversy surrounding the question of who built the monument, and a great deal of controversy about why. The most frequently mentioned candidates for builders of Stonehenge were the Druids, priests of the ancient Celtic peoples. Today archaeologists utterly reject the Druid theory, contending with convincing evidence that Stonehenge is much older than the Druids. But for several centuries antiquarians in England were gripped by a virtual Druidomania. Even today, a group of white-robed cultists, who call themselves Druids, celebrate what they contend is an ancient ritual at Stonehenge on the day of the summer solstice.

While the Druid theory has relatively few supporters today, it bears some similarities to current ETI theories, and thus a brief look at it will be instructive. Probably the foremost exponent of the Druid theory was the nineteenth-century clergyman and antiquarian William Stukeley. So great was Stukeley's obsession, that he even adopted the title of Arch Druid.

Stukeley believed that the Druids were the chief inheritors of ancient knowledge, scientific and sacred, since the time of the Flood. He not only thought that the Druids built Stonehenge, but that Stonehenge was only part of a vast interconnected network of sacred sites.

He wrote: ". . . but to our British Druids was reserv'd the honour of a more extensive idea, and of executing it. They have made plains and hills, valleys, springs and rivers contribute to form a temple of three miles in length, they have stamp'd a whole country with the impress of this sacred character, and that of the most permanent nature."

Stukeley's vision contained a strange mixture of Christianity, paganism, and nationalism. Somehow the Druids became identified with the Anglican Church, and Britain became the new Holy Land, destined to save the world from the great "pollutions of Christianity, popery, profanation of the Sabbath and common swearing." Stukeley was able to discern all sorts of relationships between ancient sites in Britain, and the placement of more modern churches and crosses.

This curious view had little appeal to more conventional students of antiquity, but it appealed greatly to mystics. One of them, a man named Alfred Watkins, was riding in the hills of Hertfordshire in the 1920s when he had a vision. In the words of John Mitchell, a contemporary admirer of Watkins, "The barrier of time melted and, spread across the country, he saw a web of lines linking the holy places and sites of antiquity. Mounds, old stones, crosses and old crossroads, churches placed on pre-Christian sites, legendary trees, moats and holy wells stood in exact alignments that ran over beacon hills to carns and mountain peaks."

Watkins spent much of the rest of his life trying to find evidence for this vision, and in the process gathered a fair number of followers who formed The Straight Track Club, which flourished for some decades.

Watkins found confirmation for his vision in the Bible, for in Jeremiah he read:

"Thus saith the Lord, Stand ye in the ways, and see and ask for the old paths, where is the good way, and walk therein, and ye shall find rest for your souls."

Or: "Set thee up waymarks, make thee high heaps: set thine heart toward the highway, even the way which thou wendest."

What clearer confirmation, he asked, was needed for the existence of divinely inspired straight tracks? Members of The Straight Track Clubs found evidence that birds migrated along these straight tracks, not only in England but throughout the world, indicating the existence of a world-wide network of sacred straight tracks, built by our remote ancestors under the direction of God himself. Others thought that these straight tracks followed the lines of some natural earthly forces that were known to the superior science of the ancients, but lost to the fuzzy-minded materialists of modern times. More recently some UFO buffs have contended that UFO sightings have also occurred along straight lines, and have found considerable significance in this.

Thus ran some of the speculation which grew out of meditating upon the mystery of Stonehenge. There is, as I have already noted, a haunting, even disturbing familiarity between such theories and much of what has been written about the accomplishments of the ETIs.

More recent, however, is the speculation that Stonehenge served as a prehistoric astronomical observatory and "computer." It has long been known, or rather suspected, that Stonehenge had astronomical significance. If one stands in the middle of the circle on the longest day of the year and looks directly down an opening in the circle called the Avenue, he will see the sun rise directly over a large stone called the Heel Stone that stands in the Avenue. That alignment is not perfect today, but it should have been so about eighteen hundred years ago when Stonehenge was probably built.

There had been speculation that there might be other astronomical alignments in Stonehenge as well. In the 1960s Gerald Hawkins, a British-born astronomer, took an interest in the subject. He made all sorts of measurements of the stones, and took astronomical data, such as where certain stars will rise and set, fed it all to a computer, and came up with a tremendous number of possible alignments. Moreover, he theorized, if the builders of Stonehenge moved a boulder around a series of holes, taking it from one hole to the next each year, they would be able to predict the occurrence of eclipses.

Hawkins' theories were widely publicized, and the general public got the idea that it had been scientifically "proved" that the builders of Stonehenge possessed sophisticated astronomical knowledge. However, it would be far more accurate to state that Gerald Hawkins and a few other scientists believe they have found evidence that this was the case. Many other scientists, particularly those archaeologists who have studied Stonehenge for years, are not nearly so convinced. In fact, some have accused Hawkins of playing a foolish numbers game, because there are so many variable measurements to work with that finding a host of alignments is meaningless. The objectors have been denounced as stuffy old mossbacks who refuse to upset old theories with new data. Perhaps so, but since many have devoted years to the study of Stonehenge, their reservations should not be brushed aside.

The popularity of Hawkins' theories, and the fact that the rather unexciting ideas of his detractors have received little public attention, have added to the general notion that the ancients knew a lot of things that they weren't supposed to know.

The old Straight Track Club pretty much limited their speculations to the British Isles. Modern speculators are willing to go further. Stonehenge is what archaeologists call a megalithic monument. That really means that it is a monument built out of large crudely finished or unfinished stones. There are many other megalithic monuments in the British Isles, but they can be found elsewhere as well. The best of these monuments outside of the British Isles can be found in parts of France. There row upon row of huge stones were set up in ancient times. Why, no one really knows, but there is a strong suspicion that the purpose was astronomical.

More daring speculators have located megalithic monuments in places as far removed as China and North America. This hints that there may have been some sort of vast "megalith building" civilization in ancient times. Perhaps this civilization was also an extremely advanced one, say the speculators. Some also contend that since the center of this civilization appears to have been Britain, then this was a great unknown "white civilization." It is not particularly difficult to discern a motive behind such theories. Nor is the attempt to prove that the white race was the mother of all civilization a new one.

Another "ancient mystery" that has excited much interest among ETI speculators is Easter Island. This small, incredibly isolated island in the South Pacific has attracted attention for two reasons. First, the natives of the island have legends about gods from the skies. Secondly, and more spectacularly, however, are the gigantic statues that dot the surface of the island. These statues are so large that many have doubted that the island's small population could have ever fashioned and moved them.

In the early years of this century there was popular speculation that Easter Island had once been part of the lost continent of Lemuria or Mu, which had sunk beneath the Pacific Ocean. It was said that the statues were not the product of the "simple natives" who inhabited the land now, but rather relics of a vanished civilization.

The adventurous anthropologist Thor Heyerdahl holds some pretty exotic theories about Easter Island. For example, he says that the people who inhabit the island originally came from South America, whereas most other scientists think they came from Asia. Still Heyerdahl sees no great mystery in how the statues were carved and moved. On an expedition to the island he had some of the current inhabitants start to carve a statue and set up a fallen one. In both cases it was tedious work, but it appeared possible.

Von Däniken visited Easter Island and came away with a different impression. With a stone implement, he tried to carve the volcanic rock from which the statues were made. "After a few hundred blows, there was nothing left of our tools but a few miserable splinters, but the rock showed hardly a scratch." One possible conclusion is that Von Däniken is just a lousy rock carver. But he reaches a different conclusion: "Alien cosmonauts supplied the original islanders with sophisticated technical tools that priests or magicians could use. They freed the masses from the lava and shaped them. Then these alien visitors disappeared."

Von Däniken continues that the natives of Easter Island may have attempted in their crude way to imitate the statues that had been made under the direction of the "alien cosmonauts," and may even have suc-

Avebury, a huge megalithic monument in England. Though not as famous as nearby Stonehenge, Avebury is even larger.

ceeded in fashioning a few smaller ones, but they certainly could never have carved the larger statues.

And what, he asks, did these strange-looking statues, with their long noses, tight-lipped mouths, sunken-eyes, and low foreheads mean? They don't even look Polynesian, and the obvious implication is that the original models were extraterrestrial. Others have suggested that such statues show "white men"—another piece of evidence that an ancient "white civilization" spread across the earth. Anthropologists offer a more mundane theory. They say that the statues really aren't that unusual. Many Polynesian people carve huge statues which they place around funerary enclosures. The main difference is that on most islands the statues are made of

The statues of Easter Island as they were seen by early European explorers.

wood. On Easter Island, which is largely treeless and thus had little natural wood, the natives used the most common material at hand, volcanic rock. But gazing at the monumental statues of Easter Island, an awful lot of people seem unconvinced of such a simple explanation.

Occasionally though, the ETI theorists come up with a mystery which should really be no mystery at all. Such a "mystery" is Nan Matol. Nan Matol is an impressive ruin located on the island of Ponape in the western Pacific. Its enormous walls, up to thirty feet high, are built of long columnar pieces of dark rock laid crisscross like the logs of a log cabin. At first glance it seems incredible that the people who now inhabit the island could have ever carved such huge "logs" of rock.

Like the statues of Easter Island, the ruins at Nan Matol were frequently cited by occultists as proof that a vanished continent called Lemuria, with a high civilization, had once existed in the middle of the Pacific Ocean. More recently the same ruins have been advanced as evidence that the people of the island once had contact with aliens possessing a technology advanced enough to carve rock into logs.

But are these rock "logs" so extraordinary that we must bring in extraterrestrial superscience to explain them? No, as it turns out, they are not. They are examples of prismatic basalt, lava which crystallizes in the earth and forms large, six-sided prisms. Formations of this type, while not common, are far from unknown in the world. The most famous of them is the so-called Giant's Causeway in Ireland. There is an exposed cliff of prismatic basalt, with heaps of broken prisms at its foot, on an island some fifteen miles from Ponape. The builders of Nan Matol need only have loaded the prisms on rafts for the short voyage. If usable prisms could not be found at the base of the cliff, then they could be broken off from the cliff, probably by building fires on the rock, and then dousing it with cold water. The quick heating and cooling would crack the rock.

The walls of Nan Matol are really quite crude, not at all the elegant stonework of the occultists' fantasies. The whole construction was easily within the realm of capability of a technologically primitive people, provided they lived in a society which considered such monuments worth building.

But photographed from afar, and provided with a narrative which didn't even mention the natural occurrence of prismatic basalt, as happened in one film on the ancient astronaut theme, Nan Matol can be made to look like some thoroughly mysterious wonder, the creation of a forgotten supercivilization. One wonders how many of those who saw the film knew anything about prismatic basalt.

Erich von Däniken knew about prismatic basalt, or at least he did by the time he wrote his third book *The Gold of the Gods.* He visited Nan Matol and, after viewing the site, still rejected the idea that it could possibly have been built by ordinary means.

He brushes aside the idea that the columns of basalt could have been transported through the jungle. In fact, that suggestion has never been seriously considered. But Von Däniken also turns down the idea that the basalt could have been transported by raft. Yet, columns of basalt have been found on the sea bottom between the quarry and Nan Matol itself. This indicates that water transport was used, and that sometimes the rafts lost their cargo.

Von Däniken's real disagreement with conventional theories of how Nan Matol was built is an emotional one. He just can't understand how people would have engaged in so much back-breaking labor. "No human beings have ever been so stupid as to submit to such torture pointlessly," he writes.

We have merely touched upon some of the major sites and monuments of antiquity which have been used to support the argument that at some time in the past, earth was visited by extraterrestrial intelligences who had a profound effect upon the development of mankind. Scores, perhaps hundreds, of similar sites and monuments have also been mentioned by ETI theorists.

Even in this abbreviated form, however, we should be able to get a good idea of the positions of the ETI supporters, and of their orthodox opponents. Leaving aside for the moment obvious errors or deliberate attempts to make mysteries, as in the case of Nan Matol, we can still see a major difference in point of view. The ETI supporter looks at something like the Great Pyramid, and says, "Puny little men with nothing more than ropes and levers couldn't possibly have built that —they had to have help." The orthodox critic replies, "My dear sir, you underestimate our ancestors' cleverness and strength. They could build such monuments without aid from the stars, and they did."

4

ANCIENT AIRPLANES AND OTHERS

The late Ivan Sanderson was a naturalist, writer, and confirmed Fortean. He liked to collect odd things— things that didn't fit in. In his New Jersey home he had rocks that rang like bells when struck, what were said to be casts of the footprint of the Abominable Snowman, and photographs of what appeared to be a string from nowhere hanging out of the sky over the New Jersey hills. But one of the most intriguing things in his collection was a small object that looked like a tiny, delta-winged airplane. There is nothing strange about model airplanes, except that the original of this one was made of gold, came from South America, and was at least a thousand years old.

The original had once been part of a collection that was owned by the government of Colombia, and had been sent for exhibit to a number of U.S. museums. Sanderson had a jeweler friend who had been commissioned to make a copy of some of the objects in the exhibit. The jeweler figured that this one would be of interest to any collector of the odd. And indeed it was.

The exhibit catalogue had labeled this and a number of objects as *zoomorphica,* meaning simply that they were animal-shaped. Most of the objects under that classification in the catalogue clearly were animal-shaped. But it wasn't altogether clear what sort of animal this particular object was supposed to represent.

It didn't really look like a bird, or a bat, or a flying squirrel—all animals that have wings of one sort or another. It looked most like a skate or ray, those flattened relatives of the shark that can "fly" through the water by moving their delta-shaped fins. There is a large variety of such creatures throughout the world, including the gigantic devilfish. The Indians of South America a thousand years ago would certainly have been acquainted with rays, and might well have made little gold models of them, as they did of other animals. And a ray may indeed be what this object is supposed to represent.

But the fact is that the object really looks more like a delta-winged airplane than any kind of ray. The most striking difference between the object and a ray is the tail. The object has a triangular upright tail. Rays may have small triangular fins on their back, but their tails are long and tapering.

While not as striking as the tail, the head of the object presents even more difficulties. From the side there is what appears to be a deep gash in the head. Why, asked Sanderson, would anyone make a model of a fish with its head cut three quarters off? This gash, he suggested, might be a cockpit. In addition the entire object has a squarish and rather artificial look.

After this initial discovery was publicized it became apparent that there were quite a number of "little gold airplanes" from South America scattered about in collections. One in the Chicago Museum of Natural

History was labeled "flying fish." Another at the Smithsonian was labeled simply "cast gold ornament." In his pictorial book, *In Search of Ancient Gods,* Von Däniken has photos of two other "gold aeroplanes" in a private collection in Colombia. But some of these later discoveries appear to weaken the case for ancient airplanes rather than strengthen it. For example, one of the Von Däniken gold airplanes shows the characteristic long tail of a ray. The Chicago Museum's flying fish does rather look like a flying fish and not any kind of airplane.

Von Däniken also cites a "model aeroplane" in the Cairo museum that was originally found in a tomb near Sakkara, where the famed Step Pyramid is located. Von Däniken says it is "accepted without question" as a model aircraft. Well, perhaps so, but to some observers, this one for sure, while the model does look like a glider, it also looks a great deal like a stylized model of a hawk, a common motif in ancient Egyptian art. Von Däniken only shows the "glider" from above but when viewed from the side, eyes and a beak are clearly visible.

In their enthusiasm to support the idea that ancient people were in contact with a technology advanced enough to produce airplanes, some of these theorists have exceeded even the wide latitude one might allow in such cases. Yet there remains that first Colombian gold object, and perhaps one or two others. While one cannot prove that it isn't a ray, one cannot prove that it isn't an airplane either. It remains intriguing.

Sanderson also located what he thought to be a small pre-Columbian model of a backhoe. The thing was found in Panama, and is probably around a thousand years old. It is now located in the University of Pennsylvania Museum. It is generally called a model of a jaguar or crocodile, and to tell you the truth, it looks a great deal like a jaguar or a crocodile or some sort of animal with large teeth, but for an animal it has some odd features, and Sanderson thought it was even more important than the ancient airplanes.

Here is how he described it in his book *Investigating the Unexplained:*

"It is a piece of jewelry made by a consummate artist; in gold containing a huge green gemstone, and obviously intended to be a pendant. It is four and a half inches long and was described by its discoverers as a crocodile, but later by others as a jaguar. It is, however, covered with mechanical devices, including two cogwheels."

A backhoe is not a particularly elegant piece of machinery. But if the people who lived in Panama a thousand or so years ago used or even saw a backhoe, or anything like it, then they had knowledge far beyond anything ever dreamed of by conventional scientists. But that bit of speculation does not solve the initial problem—is the piece of jewelry meant to represent an animal, albeit a highly formalized one, or is it meant to show a piece of machinery? The answer to that question remains a matter of opinion or prejudice.

Over twenty years ago a large selection of primitive drawings were found on the wall of a rocky gorge in the Tassili Mountains in the Sahara. The discovery came as something of a surprise, because it didn't seem likely that this particularly desolate area had ever been inhabited. As it turned out the region had undergone a climate change, and at the time the drawings were

"The Great Martian God," an ancient drawing from the Sahara.

made it was not desolate and supported a fair-sized population. The drawings themselves were rather curious. Henri Lhote, one of the discoverers, wrote of some of the figures:

"The outlines are simple and crude; the round head, in which the only peculiarity is the double oval in the middle of the face, is reminiscent of the image we usually form of Martians. Martians! . . . If 'Martians' really visited the Sahara, it must have been thousands of years ago, for as far as we know, the portraits of the roundheads at Tassili are very very old."

The largest and most striking of these figures was playfully called the "Great Martian God." This talk of Martians was a joke to the discoverers. They really regarded these figures to be representations of men in ceremonial masks. But ETI theorists have taken the light banter in dead earnest. If these drawings do not

"Men in Space Helmets," an ancient drawing found in northern Italy.

represent Martians, they at least represent spacemen of some sort. Moreover, in many other parts of the world, figures have been found that look as though they are wearing globe-shaped helmets on their heads. All of these have been gathered together as evidence that at some time in the distant past, extraterrestrials wearing space suits landed and were drawn by the people of earth who encountered them.

At the great Mayan site of Palenque in Mexico there is a large, elaborately carved stone, apparently a tombstone, that has attracted a great deal of attention. In the middle of the carving, which is crammed with Mayan glyphs and designs, sits the figure of a man. He is clearly a Mayan, not some sort of extraterrestrial in a space suit, and he wears the traditional Mayan loincloth and headdress. Though Von Däniken sees in the relief that the figure is wearing a tight pullover, tight paints, and socklike garments, it appears to me that he is merely wearing ankle and wrist bracelets. It isn't the outfit that raises speculation anyway, it is the way the figure is sitting. He appears to be semi-reclining on a couch, while his hands work levers and his foot presses a pedal. It doesn't take a great deal of imagination to draw a comparison between this figure and pictures of astronauts, particularly some of the early Mercury astronauts, jammed into their tiny space capsules.

Archaeologists have labeled this particular relief "Indian on the Sacrificial Altar" and they cite partially deciphered glyphs on the stone to back up their contention that the picture represents a sacrificial victim, a popular theme in Mayan art. Von Däniken rejects this conclusion as insufficient. "There is no definite proof that we are dealing with the usual Maya symbolism on this tombstone. We cannot irrefutably deduce from the literature that the relief contains no technical elements. It does not get us much further if we stand to attention in front of antiquated working hypotheses."

To the eyes of the ETI theorists pictures of spaceship or rockets abound in ancient art. In his book, *Uninvited Visitors,* Sanderson printed a photograph of an ancient Roman painting found in an excavation on Rome's Palatine Hill in 1961. Though indistinct, the painting shows what appears to be a cigar-shaped rocket standing upright. Of course, the picture could also show nothing more startling than a decorative column, for what seem to be two streamers extend out and downward from the "rocket's" elongated nose.

The cylinder seals, fashioned by a succession of peoples who inhabited the valley of the Tigris and Euphrates rivers in what is now Iraq, have long fascinated unorthodox theorists. Part of the fascination comes from their age. Some of them are among the earliest known pieces of art from civilized man. The themes they contain were repeated, with little change, for several thousand years. And they are very strange to look at. They are filled with monstrous half-human, half-animal creatures. In some people or gods do appear to be floating through the air in flying machines. They also contain what look like modern diagrams of the atom, or of the solar system, and some have claimed to see in them a diagram of the double helix of the DNA molecule in these ancient works of art.

But the whole style of these cylinder seals is very alien to us. While it is conceivable they do contain pictures of spaceships or diagrams of the atom, it is more than conceivable that we are just misinterpreting them.

Pictorially one of the best of the "ancient spaceship" representations is only a few hundred years old. It is contained in a mural on the wall of the Desani Monastery in Yugoslavia. It shows what is supposed to be an angel flashing through the sky inside of a teardrop-shaped object from which six extra "rays" extend to the rear. Christian art is filled with representations of angels floating on clouds and that sort of thing. But only the wildest of the ETI supporters are willing to point to such as proof of extraterrestrial visitations. The Desani mural, however, is of a different order, for the angel does look as though he is riding inside of a solid object.

The pre-Columbian Indians of Mexico, Aztec and Mayas, had a habit of representing their gods or priests as sitting inside spheres. To Von Däniken, who insists that the sphere is a perfect shape for a spaceship, this is highly significant. And he compares the drawings to the early Russian spacecraft, which were roughly spherical in shape.

Modern astronauts in their spacesuits have often been compared to ancient drawings in which the figures appear to be wearing helmets. NASA

There is, however, something about this sort of comparison that bothers me, though it does not seem to have occurred to most of the ETI supporters. They are comparing representations of their theoretical space visitors to earthly space technology, which is clearly in its infancy. Is it not logical to assume that these space visitors who had crossed from planet to planet and more probably from one star to another, had devised something better than the clumsy space suit worn by early astronauts and cosmonauts? Would they have traveled the vastness of space jammed into something as uncomfortable as the Mercury capsule? One might argue that such "primitive" devices were used only within earth's atmosphere, and that the real starships that crossed the void were never seen. Well, perhaps that is so, but the idea of a supercivilization still fooling around with space technology which is already dated here on earth strikes me as just a bit odd.

Rather than pieces of art, which are open to a variety of interpretations, it would be helpful if we could find objects from ancient times, which themselves displayed a high order of technical achievement. For example, if archaeologists had found a jet plane in the tomb of the Pharaoh Tutankhamen, that would be a highly significant, and unambiguous discovery. We don't have that, or do we?

In 1900 Greek sponge divers, who were anchored off the island of Antikyhera during a storm, located an old wreck. The report of their initial investigation was enough to bring archaeologists to the scene. They determined that the boat was a commercial vessel, probably Greek, sunk about 65 B.C. while on its way to Rome from either Rhodes or Cos. The cargo was

A gold pendant from ancient South America, said by some to represent a jaguar and others to be a bulldozerlike machine. COURTESY UNIVERSITY MUSEUM, PHILADELPHIA

mainly pieces of sculpture. But among the ruins was what appeared to be a badly corroded piece of machinery. This object remained merely a curiosity for years, until it was studied with care by the highly respected academician and historian of science Professor Derek de Solla Price. Professor Price decided that the device, which had been made with bronze plates and complicated gears, had been designed to display the positions of the Sun and Moon, and possibly the

67

planets. According to British astronomer Colin Ronan, "It was an instrument that gave the positions of celestial bodies in figures—there were pointers that moved over dials to indicate the results of its internal calculations . . . In short, this was a mechanical computer, and a complex one at that. Internal evidence also shows that it was a contemporary machine definitely made for everyday use, and not a treasure from some bygone age. We are forced to the conclusion that it pays tribute to a tradition of highly advanced technology in Greece . . . But if there was a tradition of an advanced technology in the ancient world, it did not penetrate into Western Christendom."

At a meeting, Dr. Price told his scientific colleagues, "Finding a thing like this is like finding a jet plane in the tomb of King Tutankhamen."

While the existence of this astronomical "calculator" does indicate that the ancients were far more technologically advanced than we had given them credit for, it does not necessarily mean that they were in contact with a higher culture. Such a device could conceivably have been constructed by the extremely clever application of relatively simple principles that were known to the Greeks and Romans. What is exceptionally interesting about this discovery, is that it was unexpected. We have fairly voluminous records from this period of history, yet none of them mention this apparently common device. It was found by accident, and one wonders what other technological marvels may one day turn up in an ancient wreck or undiscovered tomb.

Somewhat more controversial is the evidence for ancient electronics. In 1938 a German archaeologist by the name of Wilhelm König thought he had discovered electric batteries that were some two thousand years old. It is not clear whether König dug these artifacts up by himself or found them among material lodged in the National Museum of Iraq. Whatever the case, they had originally come from a settlement of the Parthians at a place called Khujut Rabu, a few miles from Baghdad. The artifacts were earthenware jars with necks covered with asphalt and iron rods encased in copper cylinders. To König they looked like electric batteries, and he said so in an article published in 1940. World War II was raging when the article appeared, and there wasn't much time for speculation over ancient dry-cell batteries.

After the war, Willard F. M. Gray of the General Electric High Voltage Laboratory in Pittsfield, Massachusetts, built some duplicate batteries based on the König discovery. They worked perfectly and one is still on display in the Berkshire Museum in Pittsfield.

The Parthians were the descendants of nomadic horsemen who established a wide empire in the Middle East. They were good at fighting, and occasionally fought the Romans to a standstill. But they were not noted for their technological achievements. So if they had batteries, they probably got them from somewhere. But where?

The principle of the battery was not invented, or reinvented, until the early 1800s. Were these ancient batteries an example of isolated and accidental development? Were they batteries at all? They were not in working condition when found, so perhaps König and Gray reconstructed too much. Many scientists simply do not accept the battery identification, so the problem just hangs there, waiting for more evidence, but none

Images of flying abound in ancient Egyptian art.

has turned up in the more than thirty years since the original discovery.

Stories of eternally burning mysterious lights have been reported from dozens of ancient societies. If you are willing to accept such tales as a confirmation that the ancients possessed electricity, all well and good. But stories do not constitute hard evidence.

There is an ancient Egyptian relief which appears on a wall of the Temple of Hathor at Dendera. According to the Swedish writer Ivan Troeng, the drawing "obviously shows electric lamps held by high tension insulators." To archaeologists the "lamps" are not lamps at all but "snake stones," granite stones with pictures of snakes on them. There definitely appear to be snakes, not filaments, in the middle of the bulbs. Snake stones were often used in places like Dendera, where a snake cult worshiped. The drawings do, however, bear a striking resemblance to electric lamps.

The spookiest-looking bit of evidence commonly advanced as an example of ancient and unearthly technology is the crystal skull. It is a near life-size and very realistic reproduction of a human skull, carved in pure quartz crystal. The 11½-pound skull is beautifully polished, and Von Däniken notes enthusiastically "Nowhere on the skull is there a clue showing that a tool known to us was used!" The lower jaw of the skull can be detached, and there are small holes which suggest that there once was some sort of mechanism that allowed the lower jaw of the skull to be moved.

The skull is carved in such a way that when a light is shined at it from below, it is refracted through the skull in a really remarkable and impressive manner.

The lore of the crystal skull slides over into the occult realm. It is almost inevitable that such a weird-looking object would attract the interest of psychics, since quartz crystal has often been considered to have "magical" or "psychic" powers—the crystal ball for example. Some persons who have kept the crystal skull in their homes have reported strange noises, such as the sound of chimes, bells, and the mewing of cats. Objects have been moved about mysteriously, and the skull has been reported to produce strange scents of various sorts.

But more to our point, was this skull produced by an ancient but unknown technology? Indeed, is the skull really ancient at all? There is considerable doubt. The skull appeared in about 1927 in the possession of a British adventurer named F. A. Mitchell-Hedges. Mitchell-Hedges told a lot of stories about himself, but he never exactly said where he got the skull. One often repeated tale is that he found it at the Mayan site of Lubaantun in Yucatán. Mitchell-Hedges may well have been the first or among the first to visit the site, but he never said flat out that he found the skull there. Other rumors hold that he purchased it in London.

But it could have been Mayan, for another crystal skull, similar in size though not as expertly cut, was discovered in Mexico in 1889. This skull has been on exhibit in the British Museum since its discovery. Several other pre-Columbian Mexican skulls made of crystal are scattered in other museums throughout the world. The skull was a common feature of Mayan art.

Since there is absolutely no known way of determining the skull's age, archaeologists tend to reject its antiquity. They believe that it was cut in London in the late nineteenth or early twentieth century, with the somewhat cruder British Museum specimen as a model or inspiration. Mitchell-Hedges had a more interesting theory. He said that it had originally been made in Atlantis and carried to Mexico by survivors of the cataclysm that destroyed the continent. Today some say that it was made under the direction of the ETIs.

Well, whatever its origin, and we shall probably never know for sure, the crystal skull is still one of the most exceptional carved gem stones in existence. But it is a work of art, not a marvel of technology either ancient or modern. A modern gem cutter of sufficient skill could produce such an object and a Mayan artisan could almost certainly have also. The cutting and

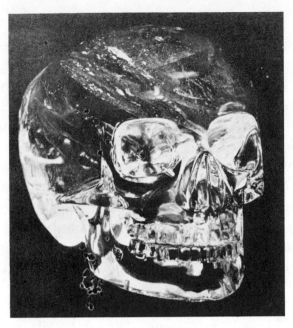

The crystal skull. COURTESY FRANK DORLAND AND RICHARD GARVIN.

grinding would have taken an enormous amount of time, but it was not too long ago that Indian gem cutters might spend an entire year polishing a single stone with a rag. Once again, we of the modern world tend to underestimate the infinite time and patience people of past ages would lavish upon their crafts, and we tend to look upon the results of such labor with uncomprehending awe and quickly attribute them to magic or the intervention of superior beings.

ETI theorists have expended a considerable amount of time and effort on the subject of anti-gravitation. Andrew Tomas says in his book, *We Are Not the First,* "Some of the most incredible tales of antiquity concern levitation or the power to neutralize gravity." Many have speculated that monuments like the pyra-

73

mids and the great Easter Island statues were built with the aid of anti-gravity devices of some sort. These devices lifted the heavy stones effortlessly. There are also innumerable tales of levitating saints, holy men, wizards, and the like. But such tales are of course uncheckable.

However, there are still supposed to be a few gravity-defying objects in the world today. Tomas mentions a large granite boulder in front of a Muslim mosque at Shivapur, India. This stone is supposed to become weightless when eleven people stand around it, touching it with their index fingers and chanting "Qamar Ali Dervish" loudly.

Tomas believes that the ancients had somehow or another learned to master "gravitational anomalies" which are "not uncommon on our planet." As an example of one of these "anomalies" Tomas gives Magnetic Hill near Moncton, New Brunswick, Canada, where cars are supposed to run uphill without power. Says Tomas, "One drives to the base of the hill, switches off the ignition, puts the car in neutral, releases the brakes, and presto the car is pulled uphill by an invisible force." He rejects the idea that there is a pocket of magnetic iron under the ground, for wooden sticks or rubber balls will also roll up this particular hill.

Tomas says that this force, whatever it is, has an effect upon people—it makes them feel dizzy or otherwise strange.

I have never stood in front of the mosque at Shivapur, chanting "Qamar Ali Dervish" and watching the stone rise. But I have been to Magnetic Hill in New Brunswick. I can state categorically that the phenomena one experiences there is neither gravitational nor magnetic, it is an optical illusion. Everyone in the area knows it is an optical illusion, and a brochure that is (or was) available at a nearby restaurant states that the sensation of rolling uphill is caused by an optical illusion created by a peculiar lay of the land.

What is more, it isn't a very good optical illusion. One does not really get the sensation of rolling uphill. The car rolls all right, but the apparent incline up which it is supposed to be rolling is so slight as to be barely noticeable. The visitors quoted by Tomas said that they felt as though they had been pulled along by a mysterious force, or that you "feel it in your bones." I felt nothing in my bones. One fellow who came to Magnetic Hill shortly after I arrived, did feel something; he felt angry. He said he had driven an extra hundred miles to see this "wonder of the world" and it was so unimpressive that he thought he had been cheated. He walked back to his car muttering "fake" and "tourist trap."

A major problem with devotees of ETIs and ancient technology is that they suffer a tendency to exaggerate, and to toss all manner of oddities into the same bag. It is really a pity, for such exaggeration tends to make serious people doubt everything that they say.

5

THE TURKISH ADMIRAL'S MAP

In the year 1513 a Turkish admiral named Piri Ibn Haji Memmed, known to us as Piri Re'is (Admiral Piri) directed his artists to prepare a map of the Atlantic Ocean and its islands and bordering lands. This map was duly painted on parchment, elaborately inscribed, and then forgotten.

It wasn't until 1929 that the map was unearthed in the archives of the Imperial Palace in Constantinople. The Turks were delighted with the find, for it appeared that a Turkish admiral had prepared one of the earliest known maps showing both North and South America. Remember that Columbus had come to America a mere twenty-one years before the Piri Re'is map was made. Moreover, this map, which seemed to show the coasts of Africa and South America in correct relative longitudes, was one of the most accurate early maps of the New World. For the Turks, who were going through an intensely nationalistic period in 1929, this was considered a major coup.

There were other reasons for interest. In one of his inscriptions on the map, Piri Re'is said that he had based the western part of his map on maps that Columbus had used on his first voyage. For centuries

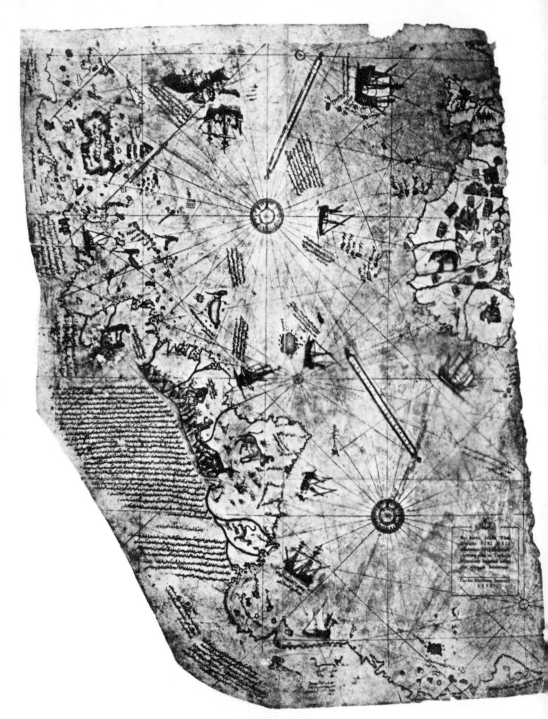

The Piri Re'is map.

there had been speculation and rumors about a map or maps said to have been consulted by Columbus. Such a map would have indicated pre-Columbian voyages to the New World. The map, however, had never been located, and there was considerable doubt as to whether such a map existed in the first place. Piri Re'is' apparently authentic reference to the "lost" map of Columbus was exciting indeed. Another significant statement made by Piri Re'is was that he had consulted twenty older maps, some dating back to the time of Alexander the Great, in preparing his map.

The Piri Re'is map created a short-lived sensation. But scholars were dubious of the admiral's claim to have possessed the "lost map of Columbus." The Piri Re'is map again slipped into obscurity until it caught the attention of Captain Arlington H. Mallery, a retired U. S. Navy man and keen student of old maps. But it wasn't Columbus that intrigued Mallery, it was something far more sensational.

At the bottom of the map South America appears to blend into a large southerly land mass. This looked like the continent of Antarctica. But, as far as anyone knew, Antarctica had not been discovered in the sixteenth century. It wasn't just early knowledge of Antarctica that intrigued Captain Mallery either. His idea was more radical still. It looked to him as though the map showed the bays and islands of that part of the Antarctic coast called Queen Maud Land. Queen Maud Land is now concealed under a thick ice sheet. The ice had overlain the Antarctic coast for centuries, and in fact, the outlines of Queen Maud Land under the ice had only been traced by a series of expeditions using sophisticated seismographic equipment in the late 1940s and early '50s.

Captain Mallery proposed that Piri Re'is had in his possession maps of Antarctica that dated back to a time before the ice sheet, which would have been over ten thousand years ago. Moreover, the accuracy of the map might indicate that the map makers had access to geographical information gathered from the air.

Needless to say, this theory was so radical that it was rejected out of hand by practically all professional geographers. However, the theory came to the attention of Professor Charles H. Hapgood, a scholar who has never hesitated to adopt unorthodox theories. Professor Hapgood, with the aid of his students at Keene State College of the University of New Hampshire, did an extensive examination of the Piri Re'is map and a number of other old maps. The conclusions presented in the book *Maps of the Ancient Sea Kings* are that at one time, probably during the Ice Age, there was a world-wide civilization that possessed a technology that far surpassed anything known until modern times. Further, he contended that this civilization was somehow destroyed, but traces of it had survived. Some of the geographical knowledge, for example, had been passed on, often in a garbled form, to geographers of Greece and Rome. It was from such information that Piri Re'is had obtained his picture of Antarctica before the ice sheet.

He writes: "The evidence presented by the ancient maps appears to suggest the existence in remote times, before the rise of any of the known cultures, of a true civilization, of a comparatively advanced sort, which either was localized in one area but had worldwide commerce, or was, in a real sense, a worldwide culture. This culture, at least in some respects, may well have been more advanced than the civilizations of Egypt, Babylonia, Greece, and Rome. In astronomy, nautical science, map-making and possibly ship-building, it was perhaps more advanced than any state of culture before the 18th century of the Christian Era. It was in the 18th Century that we first accurately measured the circumference of the earth. Not until the 19th Century did we begin to send out ships for the purposes of whaling or exploration into the Arctic or Antarctic Seas. The maps indicate that some ancient people may have done all of these things."

To bolster his contention, Professor Hapgood mentions a number of other arguments. For example, he speaks of certain archaeological sites in South America and Mexico which have been dated by radio-carbon methods as being many thousands of years old. Such dates are entirely out of line with the chronology of South and Central American history that is supported by most archaeologists. Of one of these sites Hapgood says, "We may here have a relic of the people who navigated the whole earth, and possessed the advanced sciences necessary to make our ancient maps." Most archaeologists believe that the radio-carbon dates are just inaccurate.

Professor Hapgood also contends that there is at least some evidence that people of the earth once spoke a universal language, and that all peoples appear to share a common mythology. Such views are not Professor Hapgood's alone. To one degree or another they are held by a sizable group of anthropologists, historians, folklorists, and the like. They are followers of an outlook known as diffusionism, which holds that there may have been one, or at most a very few, centers for culture, and that these spread their ideas throughout the world. Such scholars are always trying to pick out relationships between one civilization and another. They do not necessarily believe, as does Professor Hapgood, that this basic culture was a highly advanced one, nor that it existed before the Ice Age. But the desire to find an underlying thread through all cultures is a familiar one.

Now Professor Hapgood said nothing about extraterrestrials, or taking aerial photographs 10,000 years ago. These suggestions were to come later. Erich von Däniken finds the Piri Re'is map one of the principal pieces of documentary evidence for his theories. He contends that the map looks just like it was drawn from a spaceship.

This spaceship, he says, must have taken its photographs while hovering directly over Cairo, Egypt (perhaps using the Great Pyramid near Cairo as a landmark?). The picture taken from such a vantage point, he says, would exactly resemble what is reproduced in the Piri Re'is map.

As is customary, Von Däniken has "no doubt" that the maps upon which Piri Re'is based his chart were made from aerial photographs. But also as usual, scientists and scholars have plenty of doubts about such a theory. They even doubt Professor Hapgood's far more modest speculation. The majority of scholars contend that there is nothing all that unusual about the Piri Re'is map in the first place. The map is quite accurate in showing the coast of Spain, Portugal and Africa, but this is hardly surprising since these coasts should have been well known to sixteenth-century navigators. The coast of South America is also reasonably well drawn, this is less expected but not miraculous. Over twenty years had passed since Columbus' first voyage, and European mariners had already begun to explore these new lands. Central America, on the Piri Re'is map, is virtually unrecognizable and North America barely hinted at, but the majority of voyages up to that time had been made to the south.

What about Antarctica? Something that strikes even the most casual observer is that the Piri Re'is map shows the southern continent attached to the southern tip of South America. In fact they probably were at one time, but that would have been well before the time of Professor Hapgood's theoretical ancient civilization.

The mere existence of a far southern continent on the map should not come as a surprise, despite the fact that the first confirmed sightings of Antarctica were not made until the early nineteenth century. For a variety of reasons, geographers of earlier centuries believed in such a continent, and pictured it on their maps, even though they had no direct knowledge that it existed. The idea that all land masses were connected is a very old one, dating back at least to the days of the Greeks. The presence of such a land mass on so many old maps appears to have more to do with the belief that all land masses were connected into a great continent that encircled a central ocean than with any firsthand knowledge of the real Antarctic continent.

As far as the Piri Re'is map showing the coastline of Antarctica as it was before the ice appeared, this claim too can be disputed. The Piri Re'is map shows no ice on the southern land mass, and there are definite similarities between what is shown on that map and what we now know about the Antarctic coastline. Yet

these similarities are not great enough for an unmis-
takable identification. Professor Hapgood and his
students had to do a good deal of interpreting to make
the identification work.

The coastline of the southern continent on the Piri
Re'is map may just be a conventional representation of
an unknown but suspected land. Map makers did this
sort of thing all the time. That it was not covered with
ice on the map may be due to the fact that sixteenth-
century map makers could not imagine a continent covered with ice. By coincidence, what they drew may
have looked a bit like what was actually there under
the ice. Coincidence of any sort in this field is highly
suspect, but coincidences do sometimes happen.

Those who see in the Piri Re'is map evidence of the
existence of a great ancient civilization with wide geographical knowledge, perhaps gained from space travelers, also tend to ignore much of what the admiral
wrote on the map. While they like to quote the part
about "charts drawn in the days of Alexander," his
statements about "Antarctica" are disconcerting. In one
spot, in "Antarctica" he writes: "And in this country it
seems that there are white-haired monsters in this shape,
and also six-horned oxen. The Portuguese infidels have
written it in their maps." At another spot in "Antarctica"
the admiral records, "This country is a waste. Everything is in ruin and it is said that large snakes are
found here. For this reason the Portuguese infidels did
not land on these shores and these are also said to be
very hot." Piri Re'is information about the Antarctic
weather and animal life, it seems, was a bit inaccurate.

Then there are suggestions that the Piri Re'is map is
not really a sixteenth-century map at all, but a later

forgery, perhaps put together by nationalistic Turks of the early twentieth century. There is certainly no conclusive proof of this, but experts have been fooled by supposedly "ancient maps" in the past. Map and document forgery, like art forgery, is far more common than people imagine.

Adding it all up, the Piri Re'is map turns out to be something less than conclusive. Professor Hapgood himself admits, "If the Piri Re'is Map stood alone, it would perhaps be insufficient to carry conviction." To support his case he examined a number of other historic maps, which seemed to show evidence of a highly advanced geographical knowledge. But the same kinds of objections can be raised to these maps as well.

It can be argued that map makers of past ages possessed no secret or lost information handed down from supercivilizations, which allowed them to make "astonishingly accurate" maps of distant places. Indeed, it may well be that the reverse is true, and that most map makers were not really very good at all and often failed to incorporate information that they should have possessed.

We labor under a prejudice about our ancestors. We have been taught that before the fifteenth century, the great age of European exploration, there were no long sea voyages. When we find some evidence of great travels we may have a tendency to ascribe the information to the intervention of extraterrestrial visitors, or postulate the existence of a lost supercivilization. But we should, perhaps, give our own ancestors more credit for their accomplishments and their daring.

Writes Colin Ronan ". . . it is not true that there were no major marine explorations before the fifteenth century A.D. or that ancient navigators hugged the coasts, afraid to venture into the loneliness of the open sea. We have ample evidence that this was not the case, even though many early voyages were later forgotten, or at best became legends exaggerated and distorted in the telling."

The most astonishing voyages of the antiquity, says Ronan, were those of the Greek explorer Pytheas. Pytheas lived in the fourth century B.C., and was a younger contemporary of the great philosopher Aristotle, and, incidentally, a contemporary of Alexander the Great. Pytheas set out from what is now Marseilles in France and sailed to Thule, probably Iceland. The voyage took him within the Arctic Circle, and he gave the first recorded description of the Arctic conditions. He spoke of "the sleeping place of the Sun." But his voyage seemed so fantastic that many of his contemporaries disbelieved him. Only in modern times when we have been able to check out his descriptions have we begun to realize that Pytheas probably did exactly what he said he did. He was audacious and lucky, but a very human navigator.

6

THE TALE OF OANNES

The astronomer Dr. Carl Sagan can hardly be classed as a typical extraterrestrial-contact enthusiast. In the first place he is a scientist with impressive academic credentials. Most ETI enthusiasts are militant amateurs, and while they don't denounce the "pointy-headed professors" they get pretty close to it. Dr. Sagan also has something of a reputation as a debunker, particularly of the UFO phenomena. But in his book, *Intelligent Life in the Universe,* written in co-operation with the Soviet astronomer I. S. Shklovsky, Dr. Sagan unearthed one of the most intriguing legends in support of the ETI hypothesis. It is the legend of the Oannes.

Dr. Sagan and Shklovsky in no sense contend that this legend "proves" extraterrestrial contact or anything else. But in their opinion it "more nearly fulfills some of our criteria for a genuine contact myth."

The legend can only be traced accurately to the time of Alexander the Great (356–323 B.C.). At that time it was written down by a Babylonian priest named Berosus. But it is older, much older, and may well date to the very beginnings of human civilization. We have to assume that Berosus had access to documents and traditions since lost.

What first gives this legend more than usual interest is that it indicates that human civilization started in Mesopotamia, the area between the Tigris and Euphrates rivers in the Middle East. Archaeological evidence available today confirms that civilization did in fact start in Mesopotamia, with a people whom we call the Sumerians.

There is an air of mystery attached to the beginnings of Sumerian civilization. For countless thousands of years, people in the Middle East and elsewhere had lived as nomads or in simple farming communities. Their lives, at least as far as we can reconstruct from the meager remains they left behind, were comparatively simple. Then about six thousand years ago, Sumerian civilization appeared, quite suddenly it seems.

According to all orthodox theories of the development of culture, civilization should not just appear fully formed. Thus the appearance of Sumerian civilization merely *looks* sudden. It is assumed that the archaeologists have just not dug in the right places yet, and that somewhere there still exists evidence of the slow development of this earliest known civilization.

But there is another possibility, that Sumerian civilization did begin explosively after the people of the Tigris and Euphrates came in contact with a vastly superior civilization which transmitted to them many of the skills and knowledge of civilization. But where on earth could this civilization have come from? Perhaps not from earth at all. Which brings us to Berosus' tale, as it was set down by a later writer named Alexander Polyhistor:

"Berosus, in his first book concerning the history of

Babylonia [Babylonia became a general term to denote all Mesopotamian civilizations], informs us that he lived in the time of Alexander, the son of Philip. And he mentions that there were written accounts preserved at Babylon with the greatest of care, comprehending a term of fifteen myriads of years. These writings contained a history of the heavens and the sea; of the birth of mankind; also of those who had sovereign rule; and of the actions achieved by them.

"And, in the first place, he described Babylonia as a country which lay between the Tigris and Euphrates. He mentions that it abounded with wheat, barley, ocrus, sesamum; and in the lakes were found roots called gongage, which were good to be eaten, and were, in respect to nutriment, like barley. There were also palm trees and apples, and most kinds of fruits; fish, too, and birds; both those which are merely of flight, and those which take to the element of water. The part of Babylon which bordered upon Arabia was barren, and without water; but that which lay on the other side had hills, and was fruitful. At Babylon there was (in these times) a great resort of people of various nations, who inhabited Chaldea, and lived without rule and order, like the beasts of the field.

"In the first year there made its appearance, from a part of the Persian Gulf which bordered upon Babylonia, an animal endowed with reason, who was called Oannes. (According to the account of Apollodorus) the whole body of the animal was like that of a fish; and had under a fish's head another head, and also feet below, similar to those of a man, subjoined to the fish's tail. His voice too, and language was articulate and even human; and a representation of him is preserved even to this day [and to this, for there is a picture of this creature on an Assyrian cylinder seal].

"This Being, in the day-time used to converse with men; but took no food at that season; and he gave them an insight into letters, and sciences and every kind of art. He taught them to construct houses, to found temples, to compile laws and explained to them the principles of geometrical knowledge. He made them distinguish the seeds of the earth, and showed them how to collect fruits. In short, he instructed them in everything which could tend to soften manners and humanize mankind. From that time, so universal were his instructions, nothing material had been added by way of improvement. When the sun set it was the custom of this being to plunge again into the sea, and abide all night in the deep; for he was amphibious.

"After this there appeared other animals, like Oannes, of which Berosus promises to give an account when he comes to the history of kings . . ."

Other fragments based on Berosus' lost history mention creatures like Oannes ruling Babylonia. These creatures known collectively as the Apkallu, are always described as "animals," "beings," "semi-daemons," and "personages," but never as gods, though the Babylonians worshiped a host of strange-looking gods. Elsewhere we find statements like "double-shaped personages came out of the sea to land," "the shape of a fish blended with that of a man," and "the same complicated form, between fish and man."

The story does not contain a description of fiery chariots swooping down out of the sky. Indeed the creatures in this story come out of the sea. But aside from that, this ancient story sounds like a very straightforward account of contact between the human race and intelligent creatures from outer space. If one simply accepts the existence of superintelligent fish-men, the rest of the story contains no obvious supernatural elements. It is almost a textbook account of a highly civilized being bringing the fruits of civilization to primitive "natives."

It would be nice if we possessed Berosus' original account, nicer still if we had the documents upon which he based this account. The further removed from the source, the greater chance a story has of getting garbled. Best of all would be to discover the mummified body of one of these creatures, or perhaps an underwater spaceship station at the bottom of the Persian Gulf. But we have only the material which I have quoted.

Still Dr. Sagan is impressed. "Stories like the Oannes legend and representations especially of the earliest civilizations on the Earth deserve much more critical studies than have been performed heretofore, with the possibility of direct contact with an extraterrestrial civilization as one of many possible alternative interpretations."

A far older though less clear incident is recorded in the Epic of Gilgamesh, a story that does go back to Sumerian times. It is probably the oldest piece of literature that we know of. The Epic of Gilgamesh is famous because it contains a description of a universal flood that almost exactly matches that found in the Bible. Most scholars agree that both works are describing the same event, and that the biblical account is probably an adaptation of the Gilgamesh Epic flood story.

The Gilgamesh Epic also contains several incidents which have attracted the attention of ETI theorists. There is the scene in which the companion of the hero, Gilgamesh, is carried up to heaven in the claws of the sun god. Indeed, flying figures prominently in a number of parts of this ancient epic. At one point there is what appears to be a description of the earth from a great height. This account, Von Däniken believes, is too accurate to be a product of the primitive imagination. He sees it as a firsthand report of an ancient flight above the earth probably in some kind of spacecraft piloted by the "gods" or intelligent beings from outer space.

A number of ancient epics from India contain descriptions of fiery flying chariots. There are lines like this one, "Bhima flew with his Vimana on an enormous ray which was brilliant as the sun and made a noise like the thunder of a storm."

The Indian epics also contain elaborate accounts of enormous battles fought between gods and heroes. To some, like the author W. Raymond Drake who wrote *Gods and Spacemen in the Ancient East* and several other books on the subject of ETI contact, these tales are not imaginary. They are accurate, if poetic and sometimes garbled, accounts of a vast war fought with spaceships and thermonuclear weapons. The result was catastrophic for the earth. The war wiped out the supercivilization of the past leaving only legends to hint it had existed at all.

If, as the ETI theorists claim, the human race was suddenly confronted with an unearthly civilization possessing vastly superior technology which behaved in apparently strange ways, would we be likely to report such contacts as myths and legends? Would we make gods out of the extraterrestrials, and develop a religion around them? There is solid evidence that we would behave in exactly that manner.

When the technologically primitive natives of the South Pacific islands of Melanesia were suddenly confronted with Europeans and European products and weapons, they developed a bizarre group of religions called the cargo cults. The cargo cults began in the 1880s in the island of Fiji. It was a time when contacts with European ships had begun to increase. The cults were given new life during World War II, when many of the islands were used as military bases, particularly for aircraft. They continue to this day despite all efforts to stamp them out. They have proved to be a remarkably resilient form of religion.

The cults follow a general pattern. A prophet appears saying that soon the islanders' ancestors will return on a ship or plane, and they will be bringing a variety of goods like refrigerators, radios, jeeps, etc.

Followers of the cult will build a symbolic airstrip or jetty to receive the plane or ship, and a warehouse to hold the goods that they confidently expect to arrive. In some cases cults have offered to buy American presidents, for these men symbolize powerful magic.

Anthropologists view the cults as a response of the Melanesians to the changes brought about by the penetration of European goods and ideas, as well as European control. This, say the ETI enthusiasts, is exactly how the bulk of the human race has reacted when confronted with representatives of the supercivilization from outer space. We have surrounded the real events with so much supernatural interpretation that it is often difficult to discern that what is being described actually did happen.

Peoples from the mountains of Tibet to the islands of the Pacific have tales of one sort or another which speak of "gods" coming from distant places, often from the sky. But this material is at best vague and subject to a variety of interpretations. And occasionally there are other problems with these ancient stories. One of the ancient records referred to most frequently is the Tulli papyrus. This is an ancient Egyptian document that is said to have been part of the court records of the Pharaoh Tutmose III.

The papyrus tells of guards seeing "a circle of fire that was coming from the sky . . . it had no head. The breath of its mouth had a foul odor. Its body was one rod long and one rod wide. It had no voice." Further on, the papyrus reports, "Now after some days had passed, these things became more numerous in the sky than ever. They shone more in the sky than the brightness of the sun, and extended to the limits of the four supports of the heavens . . ." The papyrus also speaks of fishes and "volatiles" falling from the sky in the wake of the "circles of fire."

This sounds like a reasonably unambiguous and quite ancient account of a sighting of a spaceship. If this account really existed, it would provide a major prop for the ETI hypothesis. However, while the Tulli papyrus is often quoted, there is considerable doubt whether it exists or ever did.

The papyrus was supposed to have been the property of the late Professor Alberto Tulli, former director of the Egyptian museum at the Vatican. It had been translated by a Prince Boris de Rachelwitz. The document itself is supposed to be housed still in the Vatican museum—but it isn't there. There really was a Professor Tulli and a Prince Rachelwitz, though neither were professional Egyptologists. The director of the Vatican museum told one investigator that Professor Tulli's belongings had been dispersed after his death, so there would be little chance of retrieving the document, if it had ever existed in the first place—and that, the director doubted.

So what does one do with a story like that?

And there is worse. A number of writers on this subject refer to *The Book of Dyzan* or *The Stanzas of Dyzan*. This is said to be an incredibly ancient document that originated somewhere "beyond the Himalayas," and is supposed to have influenced the myths and legends of all countries, because it contains the purest and most ancient truths about the creation of the world and of mankind millions of years ago. From its murky passages, one is said to be able to discern accounts of contact between mankind and a superior civilization. But it seems that we only have bits and pieces of this marvelous work. Von Däniken admits that he has never met anyone who had seen a genuine copy of the book. And that is not surprising, for as far as we can tell the book never existed.

Unless someone comes up with some new and convincing evidence, we must conclude that *The Book of Dyzan* is entirely the invention of Helena Petrovina Blavatsky, a Russian adventuress and occultist who flourished at the end of the nineteenth century. Madame Blavatsky was a thoroughly remarkable character. She had a wild, nearly insane, imagination, and no scruples at all. If *The Book of Dyzan* rests entirely upon her word, and it does, then it is hard to imagine a less reliable source.

There are plenty of authentic ancient documents, myths, and legends which do contain references to what might be extraterrestrial spaceships. But this is an area in which we must step with extreme caution. The Tulli papyrus, and *The Book of Dyzan,* should serve as reminders that not all "ancient records" exist in the first place.

But now let's examine one ancient record, which indisputably does exist—the Bible.

7

EZEKIEL'S WHEELS

Of all ancient documents the Bible is the one most familiar to the West. It contains many passages which some believe are descriptions of contact between earthly man and intelligent beings from other worlds.

The most frequently mentioned of these passages is the one at the beginning of the book of the prophet Ezekiel. Ezekiel was one of the Israelites exiled by the Babylonians in 597 B.C. Five years after his exile began Ezekiel had what he called "a vision of God." Since this "vision" is such an important part of the argument for ETI contact, I shall quote it at some length. While there are many translations of the Bible, there is relatively little essential difference between them in regard to this passage. I have chosen to quote from the New English Bible, because the language seems clearest to the modern reader, and with Ezekiel, who tends to get a bit murky, we need all the help we can get. Here is what Ezekiel said:

"I saw a storm wind coming from the north, a vast cloud with flashes of fire and brilliant light about it; and within was a radiance like brass, glowing in the heart of the flames. In the fire was the semblance of four living creatures in human form. Each had four faces and each four wings; their legs were straight, and under their hooves were like the hooves of a calf, glittering like a disc of bronze. Under the wings on each of the four sides were human hands; all four creatures had faces and wings; and their wings touched one another. They did not turn as they moved; each creature went straight forward. Their faces were like this: all four had the face of a man and the face of a lion on the right, on the left the face of an ox and the face of an eagle. Their wings were spread; each living creature had one pair touching its neighbours', while one pair covered its body. They moved straight forward in whatever direction the spirit would go; they never swerved in their course. The appearance of the creatures was as if fire from the burning coals or torches were darting to and fro among them; the fire was radiant, and out of the fire came lightning.

"As I looked at the living creatures, I saw wheels on the ground, one beside each of the four. The wheels sparkled like topaz, and they were all alike; in form and working they were like a wheel inside a wheel, and when they moved in any of the four directions they never swerved in their course. All four had hubs and each hub had a projection which had the power of sight, and the rims of the wheels were full of eyes all round. When the living creatures moved, the wheels moved beside them; when the creatures rose from the ground, the wheels rose together with them, for the spirit of the living creatures was in the wheels. When the one moved the other moved; when the one halted, the other halted; when the creatures rose from the ground, the wheels rose together with them, for the spirit of the creature was in the wheels.

"Above the heads of the living creatures, was, as it were, a vault glittering like a sheet of ice, awe-inspiring, stretched over their heads above them. Under the vault their wings were spread straight out, touching one another while one pair covered the body of each. I heard, too, the noise of their wings; when they moved it was like the noise of a great torrent or of a cloudburst, like the noises of a crowd or of an armed camp; when they halted their wings dropped. A sound was heard above the vault over their heads, as they halted with drooping wings. Above the vault over their heads there appeared, as it were, a sapphire in the shape of a throne, and high above all, upon the throne, a form in human likeness. I saw what might have been brass glowing like fire in a furnace from the waist upwards; and from the waist downwards I saw what looked like fire with encircling radiance. Like a rainbow in the clouds on a rainy day was the sight of that encircling radiance; it was like the appearance of the glory of the Lord."

This sight causes Ezekiel to throw himself on the ground. But a voice speaks to him and orders him to stand up. The voice then announces that Ezekiel is to be a prophet who is to bring the words of the Lord God to the Israelites.

"Then a spirit lifted me up, and I heard behind me a fierce rushing sound as the glory of the Lord rose from his place. I heard the sound of the living creatures' wings brushing against one another, the sound of the wheels beside them, and a fierce ringing sound. A spirit lifted me and carried me along, and I went full of exaltation, the hand of the Lord strong upon me. So I came to the exiles at Tel-abib who were settled by the river Kebar. For seven days I stayed with them, dumbfounded."

This is surely a strange description, and biblical scholars have long puzzled over it. It is well nigh impossible to picture in any coherent detail what it is that Ezekiel saw. Traditionally artists who have attempted to depict this biblical scene have come up with Ezekiel standing in front of some sort of aerial chariot, containing four-headed winged monstrosities.

But the description of what Ezekiel saw also at least suggests the possibility of some sort of aerial ship or spaceship. For years UFO buffs insisted that Ezekiel had seen a UFO. Von Däniken presses that point very strongly in *Chariots of the Gods?* But even he makes no attempt to pick out the form of the spaceship that Ezekiel saw. "This experience made a strong impression on Ezekiel, for he never tries describing the weird vehicle," says Von Däniken.

However, Josef F. Blumrich, an engineer for the National Aeronautics and Space Administration took up the challenge and constructed, on paper, what he believes to be the type of spaceship that Ezekiel was trying to describe. In his book *The Spaceships of Ezekiel* Blumrich goes through Ezekiel's description line for line, practically word for word, in an attempt to pick out hints of what kind of vehicle might have been seen.

One of the greatest obstacles to regarding the description of a real object rather than some sort of mystic vision are the "four faces" of the living creatures. Blumrich gets around this problem by saying that the faces really do not exist at all:

"What prompted Ezekiel to see 'faces'? As we know from the technical description of the spaceship the gears and control mechanisms located immediately above the rotor plane are protected by a fairing [a metal covering]. The latter has an irregular shape and is provided with protrusions and cutouts. Such a combination of structural features can assume a certain resemblance to faces or can best be described by such a comparison."

But Blumrich is not entirely comfortable with this explanation, so he offers another though he considers it less likely. He assumes that the crew and commander of the spaceship had a physical resemblance to human beings:

"If we assume then that the physical resemblance to humans also had its psychological parallels, it is entirely thinkable that these beings at that time did what our pilots so often do today: paint or otherwise depict faces, birds, and so on, on the nose or sides of their fuselages of their aircraft just for fun. After all, they were intelligent beings. Should they necessarily have had less sense of humor than we have today?"

While one may find Blumrich's interpretations a bit farfetched, the vision of Ezekiel remains a very strange one indeed. The description does have a sort of a mechanical feel to it, particularly when it talks about all the creatures and wheels moving together, and of the thing arriving in a cloud with flashes of light. Moreover the mission given Ezekiel seems consistent with the ETI hypothesis. Ezekiel is told to instruct, indeed to order, the Israelites to obey an exacting set of laws laid down by the Lord. This confirms the basic promise of ETI theorists—that the superior intelligences sought to guide and direct the development of the human race on earth.

But there are at least two major points that we must keep in mind before jumping to any conclusion about Ezekiel's wheels, or any other tale of alleged extraterrestrial contact found in the Bible.

The first is that Ezekiel's vision is not the only strange or visionary part of the Bible. While much of the Bible is fairly straightforward, there are a number of obscure sections, most notably the Book of Daniel in the Old Testament, and the Book of Revelation in the New Testament. Both of these books have descriptions of strange beings and inexplicable happenings, but neither can easily be fitted into the ETI hypothesis, though attempts have been made. There is also a considerable body of visionary literature, written in biblical times, but not included as part of the Bible. So the vision of Ezekiel is not an isolated writing, it is more a part of a widely practiced literary form.

Secondly, it is important to keep in mind the fact that the Bible is a large book, from which a staggering number of wildly different interpretations can be, and have been, drawn. Blumrich and Von Däniken see in one part of the Bible evidence for extraterrestrial visitations. Others have looked into the Bible and with equally sound logic have decided that Kaiser Wilhelm was antichrist, or that the world was to come to an end in 1844. The mere fact that so many diligent interpretations have been wrong in the past should compel extreme caution.

But for the sake of argument let's throw caution to the winds for the moment and look at some of the other parts of the Bible that have most commonly been advanced as proof that the earth has been visited by extraterrestrials in ancient times.

We can start with Genesis, and, quoting again from the New English Bible translation: "When mankind began to increase and to spread all over the earth and daughters were born to them, the sons of the gods saw the daughters of men were beautiful; so they took for themselves such women as they chose." Who were these "sons of the gods"? Is it possible that the human race as we know it is a hybrid between earthly creatures and "gods" or superior creatures from space? This theory has certainly been proposed.

Other translations speak of "Giants in the earth in those days," though this phrase does not appear in the New English Bible. But all translations agree that before the Flood man lived longer, was larger, more intelligent and moral and generally superior to what he was to become. The theme is that mankind is degenerating from a higher form of life rather than evolving from a lower form. ETI theorists insist that our ancestors were vastly superior as a result of their contact with ETIs, and that everything from technology to general physical health was better in the old days than it is right now. A similar sentiment pervades the Old Testament.

The destruction of Sodom and Gomorrah by "fire and brimstone" rained down from the skies has been interpreted, as destruction caused by the ETIs through the use of thermonuclear weapons. And some ask whether the incident of Lot's wife being turned into a "pillar of salt" when she looked back at the destruction might not be poetic description of what happened to someone exposed to a high dose of radiation.

In the book of Exodus, there is the enigmatic "pillar of cloud" and "pillar of fire" which lead the Israelites out of Egypt. The Reverend Barry H. Downing makes much of this in his book *The Bible and Flying Saucers.* These "pillars," he says, are really UFOs, whose crew of "angels" are to guide and instruct the Israelites.

The crossing of the Red Sea "on dry ground," is one of the most famous miracles in the Old Testament. Reverend Downing explains it this way, "If a modern UFO were anxious to cause something like the parting of the Red Sea, it would probably use an antigravitational beam (anti-G beam) or something like an anti-G beam, to move the water back."

When the Lord visits Moses on Mount Sinai, He comes in a thick cloud, and His arrival is accompanied by an awesome display of thunder and lightning. Reverend Downing compares this description with a number of contemporary UFO reports, and finds the similarity significant.

The Lord instructs Moses, in great detail, on how to build the Ark of the Covenant, a chest into which all the commands for the Israelites were to be placed. Throughout the Old Testament there are indications that if anyone who was not properly authorized touched the Ark he would be struck dead on the spot. Von Däniken insists that the Ark of the Covenant was electrically charged.

"If we reconstruct it today according to the instructions handed down by Moses, an electric conductor of several hundred volts is produced. The border and golden crown would have served to charge the condenser which was formed by the gold plates and a positive and negative conductor . . ."

There is no independent confirmation of this statement. My own reading of the relevant verses in Exodus leaves me of the opinion that if one were to reconstruct the Ark according to the instructions in the Bible, one would have an extremely ornate wooden box, and not an electrical conductor. But perhaps Von Däniken had seen a different translation.

In the Second Book of Kings there is a scene in which the prophet Elijah divides the water of the Jordan, in much the same way as Moses, or Moses with the help of the ETIs, divided the Red Sea. Shortly thereafter Elijah and Elisha were talking, "and suddenly there appeared chariots of fire and horses of fire, which separated them one from the other, and Elijah was carried up in the whirlwind to heaven." Carried away by a UFO, according to Reverend Downing.

The bright star which led the three wise men from the East to the birthplace of the infant Jesus has long been a subject of speculation. Reverend Downing notes, "The Air Force is forever explaining to people that when they think they have seen a UFO, they have in fact seen a star or planet; perhaps the Wise Men were involved in a reverse experience."

There is a "cloud" or "bright cloud" mentioned in connection with the Transfiguration of Jesus. At the moment that Paul is converted, there is a bright light; Paul is knocked to the ground and begins to hear voices. Reverend Downing again makes a comparison between Paul's experience, and brushes with UFOs that have been recorded in modern times.

Since biblical times there have been religious "miracles." Many of these have been re-examined in light of current beliefs about extraterrestrial contact. ETI theorists tend to believe that these "miraculous" events can be interpreted in terms of contacts with a superior extraterrestrial technology. Of all the religious miracles of relatively recent times, the one most commonly associated with the ETI hypothesis took place at Fatima in Portugal in 1916. At that time three small children saw a luminous figure that they took to be the Virgin Mary. There were subsequent appearances, sometimes before crowds numbering in the thousands, for word of the miraculous events had spread rapidly. Though the luminous figure did not appear to the multitudes, there were reports that many saw a luminous globe in the sky, and that the sun began to rotate wildly. Many, however, reported seeing nothing unusual. Still the incident has been cited again and again, as solid proof that religious "miracles" are really the result of the advanced technology of ETIs.

In addition to the appearance, the figure seen by the children was supposed to have issued some highly significant prophecies about the future. It is said that there were prophecies about the end of World War I which was raging at that time, and the start of World War II which was still far in the future. There was also considerable said about the role of Russia in the future. A final series of prophecies were sealed, to be opened by the Vatican in the late 1960s. However, the deadline passed and these celebrated sealed prophecies of Fatima, if opened, have never been made public. One persistent rumor is that they are "too terrible" to be revealed to the public, for they would create world-wide panic.

Just how the ETIs are supposed to know the future history of humanity is not entirely clear. But there appears to be a general feeling among believers that the ETIs have manipulated so much of past history, for example by leading the Israelites out of Egypt, that they can and will arrange the future to suit their own inscrutable purposes.

In *God Drives a Flying Saucer*, R. I. Dione sees Fatima as absolute proof of the operations of ETIs on this earth. "If it can be shown conclusively, that one such apparition (religious miracle) was the work of saucerians, then it will be senseless to try to explain the others as something different. The Lady of Fatima incident is a case so immersed in circumstantial evidence of flying saucer origin that even the hardest nosed skeptic, once familiar with the facts, must concede that saucerians were indeed responsible."

Not everyone will make such a concession. Indeed the majority of the religious community views such speculation with suspicion at best. And yet the attempt to explain various parts of the Bible in terms of extraterrestrial visitation continues. Moreover, many see great religious significance in the persistence of UFO reports today. The "meaning" of the continued appearance of these "spaceships" is controversial, even to those who believe in them, but the believers have no doubt at all that they are of overpowering significance. A typical attitude is expressed by R. I. Dione:

"It is not out of place here to make a plea to all the people of the earth and especially to all the leaders.

Moscow, Washington, London and all the rest: you have all been monitored and are still being monitored; God, whether you believe Him to be supernatural or otherwise, knows your thoughts and (within the rule of three to a customer has tried to influence them). Before you send a man to the moon or the planets, there must be harmony on the earth. Man must prove his ability to obey God's rules."

8

CHILDREN OF THE STARS?

In 1859 Charles Darwin gave the human race a good hard kick in the ego. It is a blow from which we have not fully recovered yet. Darwinian evolution was furiously attacked when the theories were first published. Enemies of evolution are fighting a rearguard action even today. In 1969 the California State Board of Education ruled that textbooks had to include alternate theories about the origin of the human race. Well, one alternate theory that hasn't made the California textbooks yet is that the human race is the artificial creation of the ETIs.

Before we explain how the ETIs got into the evolution controversy, and what if any evidence there is to support the theory that man is a true child of the stars, we had better go back to the beginning and to Charles Darwin.

Almost everybody credits Darwin with developing the "Theory of Evolution" but that isn't quite accurate. The theory of evolution, that is, the idea that one species had evolved from another rather than each being the result of an act of special creation, had been around for a long time. It had never been a majority view, but it had its supporters, among them Charles Darwin's own grandfather Erasmus Darwin. The problem with evolutionary theory before Charles Darwin was that no one could offer a plausible explanation as to how evolution took place, what was the mechanism by which species changed at all.

Charles Darwin's great contribution, and incidentally his great heresy, was to provide the reason, he called it natural selection. Simply put, natural selection meant that those species best fitted to take advantage of the environment survived and prospered. Those less well fitted died out. The result was unplanned, chance evolution, rather than evolution as the result of some sort of grand design.

Darwin was quite aware of how disturbing his ideas were going to be to traditional ways of thinking. Being a naturally cautious man who abhorred public controversy, he tried to soften the blow as much as he could. In his epic work, *The Origin of Species*, he talked about the evolution of animal species, but barely mentioned man, saying only that "light will be thrown" on the origin of man.

If Darwin thought he was going to avoid controversy, he was quite mistaken. People knew perfectly well what the implications of his theories were for the human race. A little over a decade after the publication of *The Origin of Species* Darwin finally explained his beliefs more fully in two works *The Descent of Man* and *The Expression of the Emotions in Man and Animals*, published in 1871 and 1872 respectively.

The concept of man having "descended" from the apes, at first seemed the most shocking. "Descended from the apes!" The bishop of Worcester's wife is reputed to have said upon first hearing of Darwin's theory, "Oh my dear, let us hope it is not true. Or if it is that it does not become generally known."

Today, many biblical fundamentalists are still distressed by the idea of evolution per se. They hold that according to the Bible each species was created "after his kind," that is, separate and distinct from all other species. That went double for man. The fundamentalists quote the Book of Genesis, which says "So God created man in his *own* image." And man was given "dominion" over all the other creatures of the earth. The idea of any kind of evolution at all seems unthinkable from this point of view. That man could have "descended" from the apes is out of the question.

A nineteenth-century caricature of Charles Darwin.

And yet a more liberal interpretation of Scripture might allow for evolution, so long as it could be held that evolution was proceeding according to God's plan, or some sort of plan. That is where the really revolutionary and disturbing nature of Darwinism lies, for it allows for no plan at all.

The majority of people who reject Darwinian evolution today do so because it does not square with their view of the Bible, which they regard as the ultimate and irrefutable source of all Truth. But there are others, who are not fundamentalists, who are not necessarily even Christians, who still reject Darwinism, because it doesn't seem to "make sense." They cannot see how the whole apparently harmonious system of nature could be the result of a long series of accidental changes. Man is a particular sticking point. Human beings, they believe, are so vastly different from their nearest relatives, the apes, that simple Darwinian evolution cannot logically account for the changes. They feel that there must be some other outside force directing the evolution of life upon this earth, and especially the development of man.

Some scientists may find order and sense in unplanned nature. They may be quite satisfied with regarding the human mind as an essentially accidental development, the result of millions of years of small adaptations. But the idea of chance, and planlessness, does not appeal to most people. We try to impose an order and plan on the every phenomena we encounter—and this is where the ETIs come into the picture.

But let us be clear about where evolutionary theory stands at present. Evolution is a complex subject. There are many disputes about the interpretation of evidence, and a vast amount remains unknown. But to claim, as many of the ETI enthusiasts have, that there is any real scientific dispute over the essence of Darwinian evolution, is simply to misstate the facts. There is not.

There is some confusion over the words "theory of evolution" as though somehow or other "theory" meant that scientists weren't quite sure. In a sense all science is theory. One can hold that it is only a "theory" that the world is round, and that all evidence for the roundness of the earth is illusion or misunderstanding. When shown the first pictures of earth from space, the president of the British Flat Earth Society said, "It is easy to see how such photographs could fool the untrained eye."

In science the word theory implies a degree of certainty that it does not in ordinary usage.

Some confusion has been introduced to the subject by the views of A. R. Wallace, "codiscoverer" with Darwin of the idea of natural selection. Wallace never carried evolutionary theory all the way. He held that the mind of man, at least, stood outside of natural selection, and was the result of some sort of outside and presumably divine intervention. Supporters of ETI intervention in human evolution say that Wallace's view must be given equal, or even greater weight than Darwin's, not only because Wallace was "codiscoverer," but a less controversial figure, so he could be more "dispassionate" in his analysis.

That Darwin and Wallace apparently came up with the same idea at the same time is often regarded as something of a miracle itself. But the idea of simultaneous discovery, is more of an illusion. In fact, Darwin had come up with the idea of natural selection some twenty years before he finally published his ideas. His notebooks amply prove this point. All his friends and scientific colleagues knew his thinking. Why did Darwin hesitate to publish for so long? No one knows for sure, but a reasonable guess is that he was reluctant to face the storm of controversy that he knew his theories would arouse. When the young naturalist A. R. Wallace some years later independently came up with the same idea, he was urged to send his paper to Darwin. Darwin realized that he could delay no longer. If he were going to get credit for his idea, he had to publish it. Because Charles Darwin was a genuinely nice man, he agreed to publish jointly with Wallace, though he probably could have claimed all the credit for himself. In practice Darwin is given, and deserves, almost full credit for the idea. Wallace is largely forgotten except by those who do not feel comfortable with the full implications of evolution when applied to man. Later in his own life A. R. Wallace became an ardent spiritualist.

Wallace's misgivings about man's place in the evolutionary scheme of things, his belief that "some intelligent power has guided or determined the development of Man," has made him a favorite of many who do not really like evolution.

Max H. Flindt and Otto O. Binder, in their book *Mankind—Child of the Stars*, say of Wallace "Either he meant God and his divine power, or he was thinking of an unknown force—which leaves it wide open that *something* influenced mankind's Evolution. And that 'something' could very well be the starmen."

Pretty clearly Wallace did mean God and his divine power, though were he alive today A. R. Wallace might indeed find the ETI or starman hypothesis an attractive one.

Now that we (hopefully) have put the subject in some perspective, let's look a bit more closely at the theory of extraterrestrial intervention in the evolutionary process. The extraterrestrial theorists, by the way, do not entirely scorn the idea of evolution, they merely say that the extraterrestrials entered it at some point. What point? Well, there are a variety of different ideas about that.

From time to time it has been seriously proposed by respected scientists that life, in the form of some sort of primitive, viruslike organism, may have drifted across space from some other planet entered earth's atmosphere, where it prospered and "evolved" into higher organisms. There has even been some presumably serious speculation that earth could have been deliberately "seeded" with extremely primitive forms of life, by ETIs at some remote period of earth's history. The reason behind such speculation is that at one time it was difficult to conceive how living matter had arisen from non-living matter under earthly conditions. Yet life had to start somewhere, and so why not beyond the earth?

However, laboratory work over the last twenty years has considerably weakened the force behind such arguments. It isn't that scientists have exactly succeeded in creating "life" in the laboratory yet, but rather they have succeeded in effectively blurring what once appeared to be an insurmountable barrier between living and non-living matter. It is now quite possible to imagine how life may have come from non-living matter on earth. While it is still possible that life *did* come from beyond the earth, it is no longer reasonable to assume that it *had* to.

Next we come to what might be called the pre-Cambrian problem. There is abundant fossil evidence of life some 500,000,000 years ago, at the beginning of what geologists call the Cambrian era. Indeed there was evidence of so many different species of plants and animals, and relatively highly developed species at that, that the evidence was an embarrassment. There was virtually no fossil evidence at all for the couple of billion years prior to the Cambrian era. It made evolutionary good sense to assume that life had evolved slowly from the very simplest forms that had begun at some dim time in the long pre-Cambrian era (which made up the vast bulk of earth's history) to the point at the beginning of the Cambrian, when there existed a fair number of reasonably well-developed species. But if this was what had happened where was the fossil evidence for all that pre-Cambrian evolution? It didn't seem to exist.

The problem was a grave enough one to bother Darwin himself, who wrote, "Obviously, we have a great biological discrepancy here, one that cuts at the roots of the Theory of Evolution. If no orderly ladder of life can be found through some 3 billion years since the first genesis of primary living cells, all further evolutionary patterns in the Cambrian era and onward tend to be undermined.

"The 'laws' of Evolution, it seems, have fallen down right at the inception of all earthly life . . ."

As a solution to this problem, Flindt and Binder, naturally, propose extraterrestrial intervention, but they are behind the times. While Darwin had good reason to be puzzled back in the middle of the nineteenth century, no one should be so puzzled in the last quarter of the twentieth, for a goodly number of pre-Cambrian fossils have now been discovered. During the nineteen sixties and seventies new techniques and a growing expertise at searching for extremely ancient and simple fossils produced results. While there are still plenty of gaps in the pre-Cambrian fossil record, it is by no means a vast blank any more.

Let's step forward a few million years to the next evolutionary problem—the missing link between ape and man. Now the missing link, as everyone seems to know, has never been found. Is it possible that the "missing link" doesn't really exist because man never really descended from the apes at all, but rather was brought over from some distant planet?

Eric Norman, one of the many popular writers on ETI intervention has written in his book *Gods, Demons and UFOs:*

"Man's alleged ascension from anthropoid to human being remains unproven simply because the famed 'missing link' is so elusive. Sober scientists have declared that the bones of this ape-human will never be found because they simply do not exist. The 'missing link' could have been a shipload of space travelers from another world."

The problem here may well be more semantic than scientific. It would probably be best for public understanding of evolutionary theory if the words "missing link" were permanently erased from public consciousness. They conjure up a picture of a creature precisely halfway between the modern gorilla and modern man—a creature that looks as though it had stepped out of *Planet of the Apes*. But there isn't any creature linking modern man and modern apes, because modern man didn't ascend or descend from modern apes.

Both modern man and modern apes share a common ancestor, but for several million years men and apes have been evolving along quite different lines. We have fossil remains for a large number of man-apes or ape-men or creatures that might conceivably be a common ancestor between apes and men, but we are not really sure exactly where any of these creatures fits in in the evolutionary scheme of things and we probably never will be sure.

In order to understand why, we will have to get rid of the notion that the study of fossils or the classification of living (or once-living) things is a precise science like mathematics, in which there is one answer that everyone can agree upon. Even today you can get a pretty good argument among biologists as to whether the panda is a close relative of the raccoon or is in a class all by itself—and we have the living panda to study. With long-dead creatures all we have is fossilized bones, and often just fragments of bones.

A piece of skull, a jawbone, a few teeth, and leg bone or two will tell us something about the once living creature they belonged to. But even a complete and well-preserved skeleton, or indeed a whole museum full of complete and well-preserved skeletons, are not going to give us all the information we need to make an exact determination. So figuring out how the various fossil ancestors of man stood in relation to one another is, and is likely to remain, largely a matter of guesswork, educated guesswork to be sure, but guesswork nonetheless.

The problem is further complicated by the fact that human evolution appears to have been fairly complicated. There seems to be no clear step-by-step progression from common ancestor of ape and man to fully modern man. There seem to have been an awful lot of side branches, evolutionary dead ends. There are creatures that have some of the characteristics of man, and some of apes, but we have no way of really knowing whether they are direct evolutionary ancestors of man, or species that branched off the evolutionary line that led to man. New discoveries are constantly changing and complicating the picture. It often seems that every year or so there is public announcement that another type of early man has been discovered somewhere, and that this new find invalidates many of the previous conclusions about the evolution of man.

Supporters of ETI intervention, and anti-evolutionists in general, make great sport with all of these apparent changes and contradictions. But what they seem to fail to understand, or at least to communicate to their readers, is that the details about the evolution of man were never firm, and have inevitably changed in light of new discoveries. But none of these discoveries have served to undermine the basic evolutionary idea that man and ape did indeed evolve from a common ancestor. On the contrary, the growing number of fossil finds strengthen the case immeasureably. When Darwin first proposed that man had evolved from apelike ancestors there was not a single known bit of fossil evidence that pre-human forms of any kind had ever existed. Now there is a vast array of such evidence.

It is increasingly difficult for opponents of Darwinian evolution, be they biblical fundamentalists or devotees of ETI intervention, to claim that there is no physical link between *Homo sapiens* and other creatures on the earth. One has to make a really determined effort to ignore a great deal of evidence.

On balance, the ETI theorists do not appear to have a great deal of confidence in the idea that man came directly from beyond earth but hold rather that we are either extraterrestrial hybrids of some sort or that we are the result of genetic manipulation and selective breeding carried on by the ETIs.

The theory runs something like this: many thousands of years ago, intelligent extraterrestrial visitors came to earth determined to plant a colony. But rather than live on earth themselves, they decided to shape some earthly creature in their own image. The parallels between this theory, and the biblical description of God are, of course obvious: When writing of this theory, Von Däniken quotes The Book of Genesis:

"In the day that God created man, in the likeness of God made he him.

"Male and female created he them; and blessed them and called their name Adam, in the day when they were created."

And then Von Däniken adds his own highly unorthodox interpretation:

"According to my speculations, this could only have taken place by an artificial mutation of primitive man's genetic code by unknown intelligences. In that way the new men would have received their faculties suddenly —consciousness, memory, intelligence, a feeling for handicrafts and technology."

Von Däniken is not the only one to speculate about

genetic manipulation. This line of thought has become quite popular recently with news that human scientists are speculating about the possibilities of genetic manipulation in the near future. Nothing like changing apes into men, but still, if humans can do it, then the ETIs can certainly do it better.

Some, like R. I. Dione in his book *God Drives a Flying Saucer,* do not hesitate a moment to ascribe genetic manipulation to the ETIs. But he finds his proof for such manipulation right in the Bible:

"Starting with Genesis, Chapter 2 we read 'The Lord God cast the man into a deep sleep and while he slept, took one of his ribs and closed up its place with flesh.' The creation of Eve from the rib of Adam is undoubtedly an account of the first surgical operation on earth, and the anesthetic was, in all probability, hypnosis. Lest you scoff at the idea that Eve could have been made from Adam's rib, consider the recent findings in genetics which indicate that even a single cell from a living creature contains a DNA-coded plan for the construction of the entire organism."

Other theorists who depend less heavily on the Bible have not come to a general agreement as to when in human history this genetic manipulation took place, or exactly what form it took. Von Däniken appears to believe that it first took place between 40,000 and 20,000 B.C. But then it appears there was some backsliding, that is the new humans got in the habit of coupling with apelike animals. "Can this backsliding have been the Fall of Man?" he asks. Anyway his theory holds that the ETIs "corrected" the Fall by a second bit of genetic manipulation sometime between

7000 and 3500 B.C. At this point the creatures that were our ancestors were given a new set of instructions and civilized life began.

Flindt and Binder on the other hand, see signs of multiple ETI interventions, perhaps extending over millions of years. The various types of near-men—Neanderthal, *Homo erectus,* etc., were wiped out by the ETIs because they represented experiments in genetic manipulation that didn't work out very well.

The real emotional force behind these arguments comes not from the contemplation of the human body —for it is difficult to leave the monkey house at the zoo without the feeling that we really do look an awful lot like apes. It is the human mind that seems so vastly different. All right, we look like apes, but we certainly don't think or act like apes. Flindt and Binder put it rather grandly:

"You cannot start with ape-minds that are completely without intellect and get to human minds with their sublime thinking powers.

"It's a *non sequitur* that a dozen Darwins could never cram into an evolutionary framework."

Looking back over the presumed evolutionary history of man it seems to present-day supporters of ETI intervention, just as it must have once seemed to A. R. Wallace, that the mind of man was qualitatively different from that of the ape or of any other animal. Even if one were to admit there are no insurmountable differences between the mind of apes and the human mind (an admission that very few ETI theorists would be willing to make, incidentally) there doesn't seem to be enough time, from the first emergence of a creature that was on the evolutionary road to man, to modern man for such a large and powerful brain as ours to have evolved. The brain developed from ape size to man size in a million or million and a half years, and most of that development appears to have taken place within a period of about 500,000 years. Now 500,000 years is a long time in terms of human life or even human history, but in terms of the generally slow and stately process of evolution it is a rather brief period.

ETI theorists are also fond of pointing out that some types of early man, Neanderthal man, for example, or our own ancestor, Cro-Magnon man, had slightly larger cranial capacities, and presumably slightly larger brains than we do. This appears to dovetail neatly with the belief in superior ancestors, and the idea that man has in fact degenerated slightly since ancient times.

The apparently rapid development in size of the human brain remains a striking phenomena in the story of evolution. Striking, but not thoroughly inexplicable in conventional terms, for evolution does not proceed at a uniform rate for all species and all structures, and there are other examples of extremely rapid evolution— the horns of certain species of deer, for example.

The uniqueness of the sheer size of the human brain has also been brought into question in recent years. The dolphin has received a great deal of publicity because its brain is actually larger than the human brain. Man still has a larger brain in proportion to his body, the dolphin averaging some 300 pounds, but the difference in ratios is not all that spectacular. Study of the size and structure of the dolphin's brain has led a few authorities to conclude that the dolphin is actually or potentially more intelligent than we are. Studies of captive dolphins and observations of wild ones do confirm that the dolphin is a very intelligent animal—but most scientists believe that tales of the dolphin's intelligence have been exaggerated, and those who hold that the human race is the product of ETI genetic manipulation are quite scornful of dolphin intelligence.

"Let us get this clear," insist Bender and Flindt, "even the *least* intelligent of human beings (including idiots and morons) will be as *far above* the dolphin intellectually as the dolphin is above the chimp. The dolphin is not by any stretch of imagination equal in brainpower to humans and represents the *best* that Evolution could do in evolving anything approaching a human-like brain."

So it is not just the gross size and shape of the human brain that seem so impressive, it is the intellectual power of the human brain. But words like "brain power" even "intelligence" cannot be precisely defined, much less measured. One need only look at the subject of IQ testing, to realize that even in this very narrow area, there exists no consensus and very little common ground among authorities as to what these tests are measuring and how important the measurements really are. And if measuring comparative human intelligence is a sticky subject, trying to rate the relative intelligence of different species is a hopeless mess.

Recent studies of apes, particularly chimpanzees, have made some of the old assumptions about the difference between men and apes obsolete. For example, humans were supposed to have a true language and apes did not. Repeated attempts to teach apes to speak like people ended in failure—so it was assumed that they were incapable of such a high intellectual development. But more recent attempts to teach apes sign language, or how to communicate by the use of symbols, have been much more successful. So it appears that it wasn't that apes could not learn a language, but rather that they could not vocalize very well —quite a different thing.

One classical definition of man is that he is a tool-making animal. It was known that apes and monkeys might occasionally throw rocks, or bash things with sticks—but they simply used natural objects that came to hand, they did not alter them in any way so as to make them more useful. It was the alteration of the natural object, rather than its mere use, that is the essence of tool making. But then the naturalist Jane Goodall watched chimpanzees stripping leaves off branches in order to make probes to get ants out of anthills. Now it is a long way from a plucked branch to a pocket computer, or even to a stone knife—but the fact remained that, by the classic definition, chimpanzees made tools. This observation led the great student of early man, Louis B. Leakey, to remark that we either had to redefine man, redefine tool, or accept chimpanzees as men.

The supporters of ETI genetic manipulation also occasionally speak of other "powers" of the human mind —psychic powers, racial memory—that sort of thing. We will delve more deeply into such subjects in a later chapter. For now we will confine ourselves to the more orthodox and generally agreed-upon powers of the mind.

Are these powers so extraordinary, so marvelous that we must bring in the intervention of outer-space creatures to explain them? Clearly a lot of people believe that they are, and it is upon this belief that much of the support for the ETI hypothesis rests. But lacking any yardstick by which to measure "the powers of the mind" we must rely on our own judgment. Are we the best judges of our own mental powers, or are we hopelessly biased in favor of ourselves? Charles Darwin thought that we were, for he wrote in one of his notebooks:

"Why is thought being a secretion of the brain more wonderful than gravity a property of matter? Is it our arrogance, our admiration of ourselves?"

Actually, it seems to me that we admire ourselves somewhat less than we did in Darwin's time. There is something rather old-fashioned about the shining optimism of most ETI supporters. They speak of man as a "child of the stars," they extol our marvelous mental capacities, our sense of destiny and the great future that we have when we are someday reunited with our star-born ancestors. But such optimism runs counter to the generally pessimistic outlook of our day, when man is commonly described as "a naked ape" and we are warned that we are "natural killers" who may be "genetically programmed" for self destruction.

It is perfectly possible to argue that if the ETIs "genetically programmed" us for some sort of unknown but glorious future in which we are to join the cosmic Grand Family, then they botched the job, because we may very well blow ourselves back to barbarism, or out of existence entirely.

It has been proposed (I'm not sure how seriously) that rather than being a "child of the stars" man is really an "outcast of the stars." Earth, according to this theory, once served as a prison or mental institution for some other cosmic civilization. It was onto this remote planet that the criminals and mental defectives of this supercivilization were exiled. Earth served as a sort of a galactic Siberia. We are the descendants of these unfortunate exiles, and we have inherited many of their criminal or insane tendencies. That is why *Homo sapiens*, a supposedly intelligent and rational being, does such stupid, cruel, and downright crazy things so much of the time.

The idea of man as a favored child of the ETIs is obviously a more attractive one, but who is to say that it makes more sense?

9

THE PERSISTENCE OF UFOS

If you ask someone who believes strongly in ETI contact why the spaceships that visited earth thousands of years ago no longer do so, his likely reply would be: "But they do; look at all the UFOs."

It would probably be fair to say that interest in ETI contact in ancient times really began with interest in UFOs over the last thirty years. If you were born after 1947 you don't even remember a time when there weren't any UFOs. While publicity about UFOs tends to rise and fall rather sharply, the subject never really goes away. So today, pratically everyone has heard of UFOs, and a majority of people in America believe in them, and believe that the government is hiding something about them.

An underlying assumption of all the theorizing about ETI contact is that if human beings living in a technologically primitive society encountered spaceships, they would not know that they were spaceships. Spaceships would be quite beyond the conception of an ancient Sumerian or Hebrew or South American Indian. Such people would tend to describe the spaceships as something more familiar, a fiery chariot or a giant bird.

The creatures inside the spaceships would not be described by primitive peoples as extraterrestrials; again that concept would have been quite beyond them. They would call the beings gods, or angels, or demons, or spirits. Any technological devices that might be demonstrated would be classed as magic or miracles.

But as the age of miracles passed, people continued to see strange things in the sky. The strange things may have been the same in all ages, but the explanations were quite different. Perhaps the greatest rash of sightings of possible spaceships to take place until the middle of the twentieth century were the sightings in the United States, primarily over California in 1896–97. In 1896 people were no longer inclined to describe their sightings as fiery chariots or giant birds—they thought that they had seen some sort of airship. The Wright brothers flight had not yet taken place—that would not happen until 1903—and it would be quite a number of years after that before there would be a proper airship that could account for the tales, in terms of conventional technology. But there were balloons, and much talk of powered flight was certainly around. People knew an airship was possible, even though one had not yet been built on earth (as far as anyone knew). Today we know that manned interplanetary ships are possible, though one has not yet been built on this earth (again as far as we know). We do have our moon ship, and our planetary probes, but a real spaceship constructed on the basis of known technology is a thing of the future, just as a real airship was in 1896.

Yet on the night of November 17, 1896, a group of men were driving a team across the open plains near

Sacramento, California, when they saw a bright light in the sky and heard the sound of human singing—yes singing—coming from the thing in the sky. The experience was so strange and eerie that the men decided to keep their mouths shut about it until others from the area reported seeing the strange thing in the sky as well. And report it others did.

It is interesting to note how the newspapers of the time treated the story: The headline of the San Francisco *Call* read:

CLAIM THEY SAW A FLYING AIRSHIP

Strange Tale of Sacramento Men Not Addicted to Prevarication

Viewed an Aerial Courser as It Passes Over the City at Night

Declare They heard Voices of Those Aboard Join in Merry Chorus.

There was nothing in this account of UFOs or flying saucers or spaceships, which inevitably turn up in current accounts. Nor was there anything about fiery chariots or giant birds, the stuff of many ancient accounts. When the people of 1896 saw a strange object in the sky they tended to describe it in terms of the technology that they knew—it was an airship.

One witness, R. L. Lowry, said he had seen four men pushing the vessel by its wheels, like a bicycle. An observer standing beside Lowry claimed to have shouted up at the airship occupants, asking them where they were going, and the shouted reply was that they were heading for San Francisco and hoped to be there by midnight. Most observers on that night claimed to hear singing and talking. One said that the vessel was egg-shaped, while others said that they could only see a bright light.

This airship, or at least *an* airship, was spotted in various parts of California over the next few months. About ten days after the Sacramento sighting, the San Francisco *Call* reported that Professor H. B. Worcester, president of the Garden City Business College, and a number of guests at his home saw the airship over East San Jose, California. The paper quoted the professor as saying:

"When the ship turned to the southeast I could distinguish two lights, one behind the other. The single light first seen was about the size of an engine headlight and had more the appearance of a large incandescent light than anything else."

The professor estimated that the light had been traveling 60 to 100 miles an hour. He said the motion of the light had suggested the flapping of wings, and that the object had seemed to be descending as it disappeared.

Not far away the family of one John Bawl saw the airship lunging from side to side. It had long flapping wings and a red light hung beneath the bulky craft. It wasn't very fast, Bawl said. It was going the speed of "an electric-car doing its best."

There were hundreds of similar reports throughout various parts of California in 1896, and the wave of sightings spread in the following year.

A really spooky encounter was reported by Alexander Hamilton, a farmer from Yates Center, Kansas. He said that on April 19, 1897, an airship was found hovering thirty feet over his cow lot. The craft was cigar-shaped and three hundred feet long, with a large carriage under the hull. He said the carriage looked as though it were made of panels of glass. Inside were the "strangest beings" the farmer and his hired hands had ever seen, and they were conversing in what sounded like a foreign language.

As the craft prepared to pull away, Hamilton noticed that one of his heifers had been lassoed with a red cable from the vessel. The farmer and his hired men tried to free the animal, but they were unsuccessful, and the airship rose and disappeared in the northwest, dragging the struggling animal behind it. The following day the head, hide, and legs of the butchered animal were found in the field of a neighboring farm.

Hamilton's sighting was not the first in Kansas that year either. On March 27, 1897, a large object described by many as a "blood-red light" appeared west of Topeka, Kansas, where it was seen by over two hundred people, including the governor of the state, who made the rather strange comment, "I don't know what the thing is, but I hope it may yet solve the railroad problem."

In April 1897 Chicago also had an airship flap. The Chicago *Tribune* reported:

AIRSHIP OVER CHICAGO

Strange Vagrant of the Night Sky Sweeps Above the City—Seen All the Way from Evanston to South Chicago, Where It Disappears in the West—Comes from the Lake —Sheds Bright Colored Lights—Some Observers Say They Discern Wings—Prof. Hough Calls It a Fixed Star."

The last line was a reference to an explanation put forth by Professor George W. Hough of Dearborn Observatory, Northwestern University. He said the phenomenon was caused by sighting of a bright star in the constellation Orion. It was the sort of explanation that astronomers are often putting forth to explain modern-day UFO sightings, and then as now, few paid any attention to the explanation.

There were also reports of landings by the mysterious airship. According to the *Tribune* the thing set down in a farmer's field at Waterloo, Iowa. The airship's occupant was armed with a gun, to keep away the curious. But he insisted that he had obtained the farmer's permission to land his flying machine. He said that he was trying to fly around the world.

There were rumors of mysterious inventors who were secretly testing airships, and a number of possible airships were patented during this period, but there is no credible evidence that any of these inventors produced an airship that could really get off the ground or was in any way capable of stimulating the rash of airship rumors that swept various parts of the United States in 1896–97.

What caused the stories then? Mistakes surely accounted for a certain percentage of them. There undoubtedly were hoaxes, and newspaper publisher William Randolph Hearst, who was in his day a master of sensational and irresponsible journalism, complained, "Fake journalism has a good deal to answer for, but we do not recall a more discernible example in that line than the persistent attempt to make the public believe that the air in this vicinity is populated with airships. It has been manifest for weeks that the whole airship story is a pure myth."

So the airship of the late 1890s was greeted with the same measure of skepticism as were the later UFOs.

While specific references to a mysterious airship had disappeared by the beginning of the twentieth century, people had certainly not stopped seeing strange things in the sky. Many of the best of these sightings were recorded by Charles Fort in his books.

In *The Book of the Damned* he introduces the entire subject in his usual rather strange and roundabout way:

". . . if super-vessels, or super-vehicles have traversed this earth's atmosphere, there must be mergers between them and terrestrial phenomena; observations upon them must merge away into observations upon clouds and balloons and meteors. We shall begin with data that we can not distinguish ourselves and work our way out of mergers into extremes.

"In the *Observatory*, 35–168, it is said that according to a newspaper, March 6, 1912, residents of Warmley, England, were greatly excited by something that was supposed to be 'a splendidly illuminated aeroplane passing over the village. The machine was apparently traveling at a tremendous rate, and came from the direction of Bath, and went on toward Gloucester.' The editor says that it was a large, triple-headed fireball."

"Tremendous indeed!" snorted Fort. "But we are prepared for anything nowadays." A fireball is a natural phenomena, and Fort clearly did not favor that sort of explanation.

Fort reported that on February 9, 1932, a large, luminous body was seen in Canada, the United States, at sea, and in Bermuda. Quoting a Professor Chant of Toronto, "Observers differ as to whether the body was single, or was composed of three or four parts, with a

C. A. SMITH.
AIR SHIP.

No. 565,805.

Patented Aug. 11, 1896.

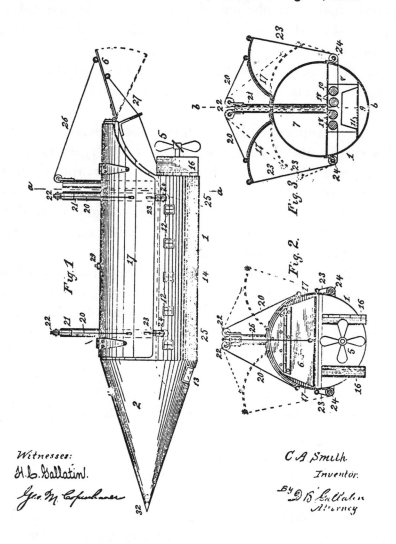

Witnesses:
H. B. Gallatin.
Geo. M. Copenhaver

C. A. Smith.
Inventor.
By D. B. Gallatin
Attorney

At the time inventors were patenting primitive and unworkable airships, people all over the United States were seeing things in the sky that they identified as airships.

tail to each part." Fort continues, "The group, or complex structure, moved with 'a peculiar, majestic deliberation.' It disappeared in the distance, and another group emerged from its place of origin. Onward they moved, at the same deliberate pace, in twos or threes or fours! They disappeared. A third group, or a third structure followed.

"Some observers compared the spectacle to a fleet of airships: others to battleships attended by cruisers and destroyers."

After Fort's death in 1932, there was no one to collect all the strange sightings in a single place, but with or without a chronicle they continued nonetheless. Then during World War II, sightings of mysterious objects in the sky got a name of sorts, it was foo fighters. Not a very elegant name. The foo fighters were strange glowing objects or somethings often spotted by combat pilots. Some enterprising American airman coined the term. He got it from an old comic strip about a madcap fireman called Smoky Stover. Stover used to say "where there's foo there's fire," hence the name.

A typical foo fighter report was one given by three members of the 415th Night Fighter Squadron. In November 1944 Lieutenants Ed Schlueter, Donald J. Meiers, and Fred Ringwald were cruising the Rhine River area north of Strasbourg in search of Nazi planes. Not long after takeoff they spotted several lights that seemed to be moving through the air. There were eight to ten of these lights, but they were too far away for the men to estimate size or distance, and they raced away at a tremendous speed. The lights appeared again briefly about five minutes later. They could not be detected by radar in the plane or by ground radar.

The crew was an experienced one, and their very lives depended upon correctly interpreting what they saw in the sky. So while mistakes are possible, the testimony of three experienced combat airmen cannot be dismissed lightly. Nor were the sightings limited to these three men. No one really knows how many pilots spotted foo fighters, because at first they kept silent about such sightings. Superior officers were not going to look kindly upon men who reported seeing ghostly lights in the sky. Finally though, foo fighters were seen by so many crews that they became almost commonplace, and since they never "attacked" or attempted in any way to interfere with the planes, the pilots soon learned to accept them. They had more immediate dangers to worry about than strange lights in the sky.

Back in America the civilian population scanned the skies nervously, not looking for spaceships, but fearing an air raid from Germany or Japan. Early in the morning of February 25, 1942, there was a genuine panic in Los Angeles when radar picked up an "unidentified target" moving directly on the city. A few hours later city residents spotted what appeared to be a triangular formation of glowing objects in the sky coming over the city from the direction of the sea. Two days earlier oil storage tanks near Santa Barbara, California had actually been shelled by a Japanese submarine. The shelling was ineffective and did little damage, but the citizens of California were extremely jittery and fearful over what might be next.

Then came the alert of the morning of the twenty-fifth. Actually the unidentified target had disappeared from the radar screens before the visual sightings began flooding the Los Angeles Information Center.

The city's alarm system went off and thousands of volunteer air raid wardens poured into the streets to make sure that their neighbors observed blackout rules, and to help people trapped outdoors find their way to air raid shelters. Searchlights scanned the sky, and there were repeated barrages of antiaircraft fire.

In less than five hours, this incident which has been called "the Battle of Los Angeles" was over. No bombs fell, and the only damage came from the debris of antiaircraft shells falling back into the city. No enemy planes were shot down, because there were no enemy planes. Despite rumors to the contrary which surface every few years, there is absolutely no evidence that the Japanese sent planes over Los Angeles on February 25, 1942.

What caused the panic then? No one seems to know, or at least no one is saying. The more or less official explanation offered by the War Department was that the whole thing was a "false alarm." Gordon I. R. Lore, Jr., and Harold H. Deneault, Jr., authors of the book *Mysteries of the Skies* conclude, "Although it cannot be proved beyond a doubt that no planes were over Los Angeles on the morning of February 25, the evidence is more in favor of unidentified flying objects.

"Thus February 25, 1942, probably marked the first time that UFOs were fired upon by anti-aircraft guns, launching the Battle of Los Angeles."

Fiery chariots, giant birds, airships, foo fighters, enemy planes—all different terms for explaining or describing strange and unknown things seen in the skies. None of these terms are used any more. Today when somebody sees something strange in the skies, it is called a UFO.

Practically everyone dates the modern age of UFOs

from June 24, 1947, when a salesman named Kenneth Arnold was piloting his private plane near the Cascade Mountains and reported encountering nine flat, shiny objects. Arnold said that they flew the way a saucer does when you skim it across the water. The press picked up the term flying saucer (though in the early days the term flying disk was also used).

While the description flying saucer may have applied to the Arnold sighting, where the objects apparently were saucer-shaped, it didn't apply to many other reported sightings. Besides, flying saucer sounded funny, and people who were serious about the subject were embarrassed by such a description. Gradually flying saucer was replaced by Unidentified Flying Object or UFO. Though flying saucer is still occasionally used, UFO is by far the more common. It has become a permanent part of our language, and people who don't know what the initials CIA stand for will know what UFO means.

The term while it sounds neutral, can be misleading. Most people who are seriously interested in Unidentified Flying Objects have identified them, to their own satisfaction at least, as extraterrestrial spaceships. The question "Do you believe in UFOs?" can be translated "Do you believe in extraterrestrial spaceships?"

While UFO buffs will generally say that the subject is a "mystery" or an "enigma" and that they are simply "open minded" my conversations with scores of them over nearly twenty-five years has convinced me that the vast majority have definite ideas on the subject.

The Arnold sighting of 1947 was widely ridiculed,

and there is good reason to believe that Kenneth Arnold was really looking at a natural atmospheric phenomena. But no matter, the sighting marked a turning point. From 1947 onward, strange things in the sky were no longer thought of as isolated phenomena, they were all viewed as a part of the general UFO mystery, and that, in reality, meant the spaceship mystery.

The UFO story since 1947 has been amply recorded elsewhere, and there is no need to give a detailed history here. As noted, publicity about UFOs rises and falls. But the number of sightings of strange things in the sky may remain fairly constant. Even if there does not happen to be a UFO flap going on when you are reading these words, be of good cheer, for you can expect that one will be along in a year or so. Predictions that interest in UFOs would disappear entirely have proved consistently wrong, and each new generation seems to "rediscover" the phenomena.

There can be little argument that a general belief in UFOs contributed heavily to the popularity of ancient astronaut theories. But does the persistence of UFO sightings actually lend support to such theories? That question is a good deal more complex.

If the ETI theorists are correct, then extraterrestrials were responsible for at least the birth of civilization, and the founding of many of our major religions, if not of the "creation" of the human race itself. If the visits are still going on, are they still having such an impact on the modern world, and if not, why not?

If fact, UFOs or a belief in UFOs are responsible for the formation of a number of small religions or cults. These groups hold a wide variety of doctrines, but generally believe that superior intelligences will descend from UFOs in order to help the human race in general or the members of the cult in particular.

The late Dr. E. U. Condon who led a study of UFOs for the University of Colorado (a study which was, and still is, hotly disputed by UFO buffs) ran across one bizarre UFO cult. A young airman and his wife joined the group, and when she died unexpectedly the group got the idea that she was not really dead, but in a state of suspended animation. Moreover they were convinced that the space people would come down in a UFO and revive her. So instead of burying the body they wrapped it up and stored it in a garage. After a few weeks a suspicious neighbor alerted the police.

In the late 1950s psychologists infiltrated a group of UFO cultists who believed that the world would be destroyed, but that they would be saved by being carried off in a UFO. The group spent a cold winter's night waiting out in one of the member's backyard for the UFO to descend. It didn't, but the members were surprisingly undiscouraged by the failure.

Most modern-day UFO cults base their beliefs on some sort of revelation. That is the cult leaders claim to be in telepathic or psychic contact with the space people, and are receiving instructions directly from them. The messages that such "contactees" receive from the space people sound an awful lot like the messages that mediums or sensitives or psychics of earlier generations received from the spirits, or "the hidden masters." It looks and sounds as though the spiritualism and occultism of the past has simply been provided with a shiny new name—and even the name isn't so new any more.

Three photographs of a UFO taken by highway inspector Rex Heflin in Santa Ana, California, early on the afternoon of August 3, 1965.

There is not much one can do with such claims; one either accepts them or rejects them. They lend no tangible support to the ETI hypothesis. The crux of theories like those of Von Däniken are physical contacts between ETIs and human beings, not telepathic or psychic contact. Ezekiel didn't have a vision, he wasn't describing pictures in his head—he was describing a real spaceship, says the ETI believers. And the extraterrestrials who stepped out of that spaceship gave him real information about what was going to happen in the future. If we have only telepathic contact, then the whole argument falls apart.

So we must turn to the stories of those who claim to have actually seen spaceships and their occupants up close. Since 1947 there have been hundreds and hundreds of such stories reported. They vary from stories of an individual who says he merely glimpsed a UFO occupant through a window, or got a brief look when the ship landed and its occupant stepped out, to those who claim to have had long and detailed conversations with the extraterrestrials, and even to have taken trips back to the extraterrestrials' home planet aboard the spaceships.

But all of these stories share one common characteristic—inconclusiveness—they are impossible to check out. Let me illustrate with a personal example. A few years ago I appeared on a radio program with a man who claimed that he had repeatedly contacted extraterrestrials near his home, a small town in West Virginia. Further, he claimed that the extraterrestrials had taken him on several trips through space in their craft.

The fellow had been going around the country repeating his story on the lecture circuit and radio and

TV programs, and he had gained a modest degree of fame from it. He looked like an ordinary sort of guy, and he told his tale in a straightforward and rather convincing manner. He did not gibber and drool, as a madman is supposed to, nor was he shifty and nervous. In short, from simply looking at him and talking to him there was no obvious reason to believe that he was not telling the absolute truth. There are those who claim that they know when someone is telling the truth just by looking them square in the eye. I looked this fellow square in the eye, and he looked right back at me, and I think that I must have looked more like the liar than he. In any event this eyeball-to-eyeball contact did not give me any indication that he was not telling the absolute truth.

Still the story was so fantastic that I doubted it, and said so over the air. The man's response was that he had at least fifteen eyewitnesses in his home town who would vouch for the truth of what he had said, for they too had seen the spaceships. Fifteen witnesses to a UFO landing is an impressive number—perhaps even a record. All I had to do, this man said, was to come down to West Virginia with him and meet his witnesses. I couldn't just go flying down to West Virginia, but I did want to get in touch with the witnesses. So the man said he would provide me with appropriate names and addresses. With that the show was over, and I'm sure that many listeners were impressed with the man's story and his apparently genuine offer to supply eyewitness testimony to back it up. If they had been in the studio, however, they would have gotten a different impression, because he beat it out the door without ever giving me a single name.

But I was persistent. After all, I thought, the fellow might have really been in a hurry, and forgotten to give me the names. I traced him to his hotel room the next day, and after some difficulty did get the names and addresses of his fifteen witnesses. They included the town's mayor, a newspaper reporter, and a radio newsman as well as a psychiatrist who was living in the town. It was a list of good, solid citizens, and I wrote all of them requesting further information.

The results of my fifteen letters were interesting. One man called me up almost immediately and said, in effect, "Is that nut still using my name? If he ever comes back to this town we're going to lynch him."

A reply from the newspaper reporter stated that he had only reported what the man had told him, but had absolutely no independent evidence to support the story, and that he, the reporter, had not seen anything. I received no response at all to four of the letters and the majority—nine out of the fifteen—were returned to me stamped "addressee unknown." All of these letters had been sent to a small town, so that even if the individual in question had moved, or the address had been wrong, the letter probably would have been delivered anyway. Besides, I had been assured that the addresses were current. I think it was fair to conclude that nine of the witnesses simply did not exist, and the others hadn't seen anything or were not willing to talk about it. Indeed in one case the "witness" asserted the story was a flat-out lie.

That does not represent stunning support for the man's story about being taken aboard a UFO. Of course, this was only one of many reported contacts

146

with ETIs that have been made since 1947—but the quality of the evidence is, I am afraid, rather typical.

How about physical evidence? ETI theorists claim that the space people gave the ancients various sorts of advanced technological devices that they could not have made on their own. Are they still passing out "trinkets" to the natives? No one as far as I know has produced a working ray gun, or an anti-gravity machine or any other "advanced" device, proffered by the ETIs. There are innumerable reports of pieces of metal or other material's "unknown to science" found in association with UFO sightings. I have personally tried to track down a number of such reports. But it invariably turns out that the "unearthly" material is really something quite ordinary—like aluminum foil, or that it has "disappeared" before it can be analyzed. Frequently I have been told that the mysterious substance was turned over to people who called themselves "government agents" and then never returned. Later the government denied that they had ever sent agents, or indeed had any interest at all in the material.

There have been so many stories of vital evidence being lost or spirited away mysteriously that one would think UFO buffs would finally learn to hang onto the stuff—but they never seem able to. And this inevitably leads to the suspicion that there never was any unusual material in the first place.

Rumors that a "revelation" is about to be made regularly sweep the UFO field. In late 1974 the news that NBC was planning a special on UFOs set off a flurry of such rumors. TV specials on UFOs are not unknown, but this one was supposed to be different.

NBC was finally going to "reveal the truth," so said the rumors, anyway. Part of the "truth" was that a spaceship had crashed in the southwest, and that the wreckage of the ship and the bodies of the UFO pilots had been found by the Air Force. This evidence had been locked away for many years, because the Air Force was afraid that the public would panic if they found out that we really were under observation by creatures from another planet.

I had been hearing one variation or another of that particular story for a very long time. I received a number of calls from UFO buffs that I know throughout the country. When I expressed my reservations they assured me that the revelation was going to be made on nationwide television without fail. So I watched the show. It was fairly standard TV documentary fare—not bad. But there was absolutely no revelation. Indeed the show came down fairly heavily on the negative side of the UFO question. I can't say I was surprised.

Ancient spaceships have been credited with such major events as the destruction of Sodom and Gomorrah and leading the Children of Israel out of Egypt. Have they done anything earth-shaking in modern times? They have been associated with—hence blamed for—some major power failures, and mysterious disappearances. But once again the evidence is not within hailing distance of being convincing.

How good are members of UFO crews at prophecy? If many ancient myths and legends are based upon contact with the crews of spaceships, then it appears that the ETIs often stepped out of the spaceships to tell people what was about to happen in the future.

There are today plenty of contactees who claim that they have received prophetic revelations or information from the space people. If people who claim to be in contact with ETIs do possess authentic prophetic information, this would certainly constitute a very strong argument in favor of the reality of ETI contact.

But alas, prophecy, whether it comes from the spirits or from outer space, all appears to suffer one common failing—it is fuzzy, and the meaning of the prophetic utterance only seems to become clear after the prophesied event has taken place. When the prophetic statement is clear and definite, it is all too often definitely wrong.

A few years back, when I was working on a magazine, I was called by a friend who was much involved with UFO investigation. He was very much upset, because UFO contactee circles were abuzz with a highly disturbing rumor. Several prominent contactees had been informed by the space people that the earth had passed through a high radiation belt, which had caused a genetic change in the human reproductive system. As a result all the babies born for the next generation would be boys. This process, said the contactees had already begun, and only boys had been born in New York City hospitals for two weeks. The government, however, was hushing the whole thing up in order to avert panic.

My friend wanted me to check with the maternity wards of city hospitals, figuring that perhaps some nurse might tip me off to "the truth." He was somewhat embarrassed at making this request, and kept on repeating "I know this sounds nuts." It sure did. But he was so dead serious, and so completely sure of what he was saying that after a while I became a bit concerned myself.

I actually called the maternity wards of half a dozen hospitals, with some sort of excuse about doing an article on the ratio of the sexes in the coming generation. When I asked for the relative percentage of boys and girls born over the last few weeks, the invariable reply was, about fifty-fifty as usual.

I don't think anyone suspected why I was really calling, and I'm glad. The replies I received were casual—no nervous assurances that everything was normal, and no suspiciously ambiguous statements. I began to feel pretty foolish and gave up the project. As we now all know the contactees' information had been false—and I have never tried to check out any more of their predictions.

10

DISAPPEARANCES, APPEARANCES, AND EXPLOSIONS

A variety of strange and mysterious happenings have been attached more or less loosely to the ETI visitation theory. In this chapter we are going to bring a few of them together and examine their possible significance.

Most people interested in the strange and the bizarre have been fascinated by the subject of mysterious disappearances. Certainly the most widely discussed disappearance of modern times was what happened on December 5, 1945. That was the day in which a squadron of five planes disappeared without a trace somewhere off the coast of Florida. It was within the area that has come to be called the Bermuda Triangle.

That story is so well known that it does not bear repeating in any detail. It is sufficient to say that the five TBF Avengers took off on a routine training flight. The weather was good, and the group was under the leadership of a qualified flight instructor. About two hours after takeoff, the Naval Air Station at Fort Lauderdale, Florida, picked up some strange radio messages from the group. The messages indicated that the men were lost and confused. The planes' compasses didn't seem to be functioning properly. There was more rather confused and garbled conversation between the planes, and then nothing. The five planes were never seen or heard from again.

A massive sea and air search was mounted. During the search one of the search planes also disappeared. An oil slick and wreckage may have indicated where the missing search plane went down, but not a single trace was found of the five TBF Avengers or their fourteen crew members. It is a mystery of the air and one that has not been solved to this day.

Two years after the disappearance of the planes the UFO or flying-saucer "mystery" arose, and UFO devotees quickly began linking UFOs to this and many other mysterious disappearances. And the rumors started. In his book *Flying Saucers Are Watching Us,* Otto Binder states:

"However, it was later reported, though officially denied by the Navy, that one airman in a rubber raft had returned, babbling about 'weird airships' that had abducted the others and that only he had managed to bail out and escape. This airman was then taken into Naval custody and spirited away—that is, held incommunicado from the public and all reporters.

"Certain UFO investigators have followed up leads to this man but seemingly failed to find him, or to get him to tell the full story. And so the mystery remains unsolved to this day, except perhaps for a report hidden away in Naval archives."

The mystery remains unsolved to this day, as well. There is simply no evidence whatsoever that any survivor was found from the disappearance, much less one babbling about weird airships. As we already noted, the UFO field is filled with rumors of this type. There is always something being hidden in some secret file. Just how the "UFO investigators" manage to find out about this "secret information" is rarely made clear. But not a single one of these rumors—and there have been hundreds of them floated over the past quarter century —has ever turned out to be anything more than just a rumor.

So this is a typical UFO rumor. But there is something quite interesting about it. When one mentions the disappearance of the five planes today, the phrase "Ber-

Five TBF Avenger torpedo bombers similar to those which disappeared over the Bermuda Triangle on December 5, 1945. U. S. NAVY PHOTOGRAPH

muda Triangle" immediately comes to mind. For this is certainly the most mysterious of the disappearances within the Bermuda Triangle. Early UFO buffs like Binder didn't talk about the Bermuda Triangle, because the Bermuda Triangle hadn't been invented yet.

The phrase Bermuda Triangle was first coined by the writer Vincent Gaddis in an article for *Argosy* magazine in 1964—nearly twenty years after the planes had disappeared. What Gaddis had done was list a number of disappearances which had taken place in roughly the same region, a triangular patch of sea that has one point on the coast of Florida, another at Puerto Rico, and a third at Bermuda. Other danger zones in which mysterious disappearances are supposed to take place have also been identified. Ivan Sanderson thought he had located about ten of them.

We will leave aside extensive examination of whether mysterious disappearances actually do take place more frequently in the Bermuda Triangle than elsewhere. Critics say that people like Sanderson and Gaddis are making mysteries where none really exist. They contend that planes and ships disappear all the time, but that doesn't mean that there is anything bizarre about any particular disappearance. It merely means that we don't have all the information we should. As far as there being any special "areas" for disappearances, the critics say that this is an illusion created by sensational writers. They take one puzzling disappearance, like the one of the five planes in the Bermuda Triangle, and then tack a lot of other disappearances, which in many cases may not be mysterious at all. This creates a grand "enigma" out of a series of smaller problems.

That is what the critics say. ETI theorists, however,

are convinced that such disappearances are genuinely mysterious. How do they explain them? Otto Binder said:

"Serious UFOlogists no longer disbelieve these tales of aerial kidnappings by flying saucers. Too many aircraft —several have been airliners with dozens of people aboard —have vanished like ghosts, wreckage or bodies never having been found.

"The weight of evidence is quite strong that UFO's are indeed capturing planes whole, here and there." He might have added ships too.

Mysterious disappearances had also fascinated Charles Fort. He had perused accounts of hundreds, perhaps thousands of them. And many of these accounts appear in his books. One that took place on July 24, 1924, is typical. It concerns a couple of British airmen who had set out on a routine reconnaissance mission over a desert in the Middle East. Fort picks up the story:

"The men did not return, and they were searched for. The plane was soon found, in the desert. Why it should have landed was a problem. 'There was some petrol left in the tank. There was nothing wrong with the craft. It was, in fact, flown back to the aerodrome.' But the men were missing. 'So far as can be ascertained, they encountered no meteorological conditions that might have forced them to land.' There was no marks to indicate that the plane had been shot at. There may be some way, at present exclusively known, of picking an aeroplane out of the sky. According to the rest of this story, there may be some such way of picking men out of a desert.

"In the sand, around the plane, were seen the footprints of Day and Stewart [the plane's crew]. 'They were traced, side by side, for some forty yards from the machine. Then, as suddenly as if they had come to the brink of a cliff, the marks ended.'"

Fort was also interested in people who disappeared repeatedly, like Professor George A. Simcox, Senior Fellow of Queen's College, Oxford. Professor Simcox went for a walk on August 28, 1905, and never returned. Fort comments, "Several times before, Professor Simcox had attracted attention by disappearing. The disappearance at Ballycastle was final."

Fort speculated, though it is hard to tell how seriously, on teleportation, that is, the instantaneous transference of matter from one place to another, as an explanation for some of these mysterious disappearances and reappearances. Teleportation would be an excellent method for getting the ETIs here from the cosmos.

Fort was also interested in mysterious appearances, people who seemed to pop up out of nowhere. Fort's interest in Kaspar Hauser was alluded to in Chapter I. Hauser was a German lad of about eighteen who walked into the city of Nuremberg one Monday in May 1828. He could only speak a few words of German, and to all appearances was even unacquainted with such things as the flame on a candle, for he burned his hand, though he was able to write his name.

After he learned the language Kaspar Hauser told a strange story about having been kept in a dark room for all the years before his sudden appearance. There were all sorts of inconsistencies in Hauser's account. A lot of people then and now believe he was an impostor, and quite mad as well.

The manner of his death was as controversial as his

life. In 1833 Hauser claimed that he had been stabbed by a mysterious assassin in the park. At first the wound did not appear serious, but it turned out to be so, and Kaspar Hauser died of it.

The problem with the assassination was that it had snowed before Hauser had entered the park. When the ·spot where the attack was supposed to have taken place was examined, only Hauser's own footprints were found. Many concluded, not unreasonably, that Hauser's wound was self-inflicted. But some doctors testified that it could not possibly have been self-inflicted. So Fort had apparently toyed with the idea that Hauser was an emissary from an unknown world who was mysteriously assassinated because "he knew too much."

Cagliostro was another of Fort's interests. Cagliostro was an eighteenth-century occultist who appeared

Kaspar Hauser.

rather mysteriously in Europe, claiming all sorts of secret knowledge. He became popular in aristocratic circles in France before the revolution, and was supposed to have been a friend of the queen, Marie Antoinette.

Cagliostro was accused in a plot to steal the Queen's necklace (an act of which he was apparently perfectly innocent) and exiled. He wandered about Europe living by his wits and wound up in Rome where he incurred the extreme displeasure of the Church. He was imprisoned under harsh conditions, and died there, though the manner and time of his death are not exactly known.

Confirmed occultists today still revere Cagliostro as some sort of a representative of the Hidden Masters who are supposed to rule the world. Some claim that he is immortal and still lives somewhere. Every once in a while there is an occultist who says he or she has met Cagliostro recently. Most non-occultists think that Cagliostro was identified as Joseph Balsamo, an Italian swindler, who adopted a false name and had a reasonably successful career hoaxing gullible and stupid aristocrats.

Fort, however, was not so sure the story was quite that ordinary. "Cagliostro appeared, and nothing more definite can be said of his origin. He rose and dominated, as somebody from Europe, if transported to a South Sea Island, might be expected to capitalize his superiority." Fort stops short of saying that Cagliostro was a representative of a superior civilization, but the implication is clear enough.

If extraterrestrials are somehow responsible for all or some of the mysterious disappearances reported by Fort and others, what possible reason might they have for such kidnapings? A number of speculations have been offered on this point. The most common is that human beings are being whisked away to serve as "specimens" in some cosmic laboratory or zoo.

There are a number of reports by contactees of being taken aboard UFOs and examined before being released. You might think that after all these centuries the ETIs would have a pretty good idea of what human beings were built like. But—disturbing thought —perhaps we are used in "terminal experiments" like white mice or experimental monkeys. Scientists are always having to go back to the jungle to get more monkeys for their cancer tests. Perhaps when monkeys disappear their companions feel much the way we do in the face of mysterious disappearances. There have even been suggestions that human beings are a choice item of diet on the extraterrestrial menu. It is difficult to know whether such thoughts are serious suggestions or simply nightmares. But they have been offered.

These ideas, however, surely do not square away with the concept of benevolent ETIs guiding the human race toward a great destiny.

Another suggestion is that human beings are being kidnaped for breeding purposes. If one accepts the idea that the human race is some sort of hybrid between spacemen and ape, this idea makes a bit of sense. There are numerous reports of individuals being forced to have sexual relations with extraterrestrials from UFOs.

The April 2, 1967, issue of the tabloid *National Tattler* contained a headline—"I WAS SEDUCED BY A FLYING SAUCERMAN!"

But here we must draw the line. The suspicion that

such tales are pure invention, an attempt to mix sex and UFOs in one salable package is too strong to ignore. There has never been anything vaguely resembling a reasonable facsimile of evidence that such events ever took place outside of the mind of the person who wrote the story in the first place.

And yet, some ETI theorists, while a bit hesitant, say that we should not ignore such accounts completely. Writes Otto Binder, "It must be remembered that these sensation-filled sheets also carry quite serious and sober scientific articles, glimpses into the space-age future, and such. And despite their shock approach to their regular human-life stories, the cases are based on solid facts." Occasionally ETI enthusiasts will then go on to relate medieval cases of men and women being seduced by demons. Read extraterrestrials for demons, and you have a long history of such things.

Fort had apparently wondered whether certain individuals had somehow learned the "secret of teleportation." More recently there has been speculation that "the government," that vague collection of sinister earthly powers, might not possess "the secret."

In a variety of books on ETIs one runs across references to "the Philadelphia Experiment." This was supposed to have taken place in November 1943. A Navy ship is said to have disappeared instantly from its moorings in the Philadelphia Navy Yard and reappeared at the same moment in the harbor at Norfolk, Virginia, a thousand miles away. According to the stories this was to have been a test of an "invisibility technique." But instead of becoming invisible the ship was teleported to Norfolk. As a result of the experiment most of the crew either disappeared, or "died raving lunatics."

Writes Robert Charroux, in his book *The Gods Unknown:* "All documents relating to the Philadelphia Experiment were lodged among top-secret files in the American Navy and an embargo placed on the subject. Consequently, the mystery cannot now be solved, since documents that might shed light on it are not open to public inspection."

How then did Charroux and all the others find out about it if it is top secret? The source was M. K. Jessup, a man of some scientific training and an enthusiastic UFO buff who had written several books on the subject. Jessup said that he got his information from mysterious letters written to him by a man called Carlos Allende or Carl Allen. No one knew who this fellow was, and the Navy not only refused to confirm the Philadelphia Experiment, spokesmen barely concealed their annoyance that such a silly story could be given any credence at all.

Jessup and his letter were the only source of information for the Philadelphia Experiment, and the story might have died, if Jessup had not. In 1959 Jessup was found dead. Suicide, said the official investigation. Mysterious circumstances, retorted UFO buffs. They hinted he was silenced because he, like so many others, "knew too much."

There is, however, good solid evidence that M. K. Jessup committed suicide, and there is nothing mysterious about his death. He was a strange and severely depressed man. He had often talked of suicide. Shortly before his death he tried to arrange for a seance to be conducted on an all-night radio show. The purpose was so that Jessup could speak to the radio audience from beyond the grave after he killed himself.

Repeated references to something like the Philadelphia Experiment can have an effect on the uninitiated. At first the story is dismissed as absurd—too unbelievable even to be considered. But then one hears of it again and again. And after a while you may begin to wonder if there isn't "something" to it after all. Could anyone have simply "made up" such an incredible tale?

But after a quarter of a century of exposure to tales of bizarre phenomena, one becomes a bit skeptical, even cynical of tales of this sort. They are always around. There are constant reports of mysterious government experiments and whatnot that are being hushed up. Such reports never come to anything.

Only those thoroughly addicted to conspiratorial thinking continue to believe the stories. This is a bad age in which to try to deny government conspiracies. We have found out that there have, in fact, been quite a number of them. But the conspiracies have never been airtight. Someone always talked; often many people talked. In the Philadelphia Experiment we are asked to believe that everyone who witnessed it, everyone who treated those poor raving lunatics who survived, not to mention those who are supposed to have planned the experiment, have kept perfectly silent. That the only "leak" was an unknown letter writer who chose to communicate his information to an unstable UFO buff. You may believe in such conspiracies if you like—but it is too elaborate for me. I assume that most people simply can't keep their mouths shut very long.

Unlike the Philadelphia Experiment, which is a dubious mystery at best, the 1908 Siberian explosion is a genuine mystery—perhaps one of the most mysterious things that has ever happened on this earth in historical times.

At the end of June 1908, something hit a forested area of Siberia. The area was so remote that it was years before the outside world had more than a hint of what had happened. At the time seismographs in various parts of the world indicated that something had happened—it was assumed that a minor earthquake had taken place, though earthquakes were virtually unknown in that part of Siberia.

When outsiders finally visited the site of the explosion in 1927, they found a circular area of from twenty to twenty-five miles in diameter which had been devastated. Tribesmen who lived in the region spoke of a pillar of fire, and of the terror of the shock waves set off by the explosion.

The first assumption was that a huge meteorite had fallen on Siberia. But examination of what should have been the impact center revealed no trace of the meteorite. Nor was there a conventional impact crater. A host of other explanations have been put forward. Various authorities have assigned the responsibility for the disaster to a comet which vaporized on impact, a meteorite made of anti-matter, and a dust-sized piece of a "black hole." Black holes are theoretical collapsed stars so dense that not even light can escape from them. A tiny particle of such a dense object could, in theory, create a tremendous explosion if it hit the earth. But since both black holes and anti-matter are still in theory stage, the comet explanation commands the most support among scientists at the present time.

Among ETI theorists there is a different explanation, a nuclear-powered spaceship exploded near the earth's surface in 1908. There are two supports for such a theory. First is the general tendency to attribute everything unexplained to the actions of the extraterrestrials. The second support for the theory is a report that in 1960 a group of Russian scientists visited the region and found that it was highly radioactive. This would have been the result of fallout from the doomed spaceship's nuclear power source.

But the tale of the Russian scientists is apparently something of an exaggeration. The 1960 visitors were not scientists but amateurs, and there is no scientific confirmation of the excessive radioactivity readings. This tale, like so many wondrous science tales that have come out of Russia in recent years, is hard to pin down.

But in any case the 1908 explosion remains a genuine mystery—and a fascinating one.

11

OTHER PLACES, OTHER TIMES

If you have become slightly bored with the idea that UFOs come from outer space, perhaps a theory of Ray Palmer's will intrigue you. Palmer was (and still is) an editor and publisher of science-fiction and other offbeat magazines. He was one of the earliest and most effective publicists of the entire UFO phenomena. At first he championed the outer-space idea, but after a whole flock of others picked up on the same theme, Palmer moved on to other explanations.

By 1959 Palmer was insisting that he could: ". . . prove that the flying saucers are native to the planet earth; that the government of more than one nation (if not all of them) know this to be a fact; that a concerted effort is being made to learn all about them and to explore their native land; that the facts already known are considered so important that they are the world's top secret . . ."

Where on earth could the flying saucers—a term that Palmer prefers to UFOs—come from? Palmer quickly eliminates the Mato Grosso of Brazil and the Tibetan mountains, two spots which had often been mentioned as the locations of UFO "bases." He does, however, think that the North and South poles deserve more attention. Not that the saucers come from the poles themselves, but rather that there are large holes in the polar region and that the saucers fly out of these holes from inside the earth. The earth, he says, is shaped rather like a doughnut.

"The evidence is extremely strong, and amazingly prolific in scope and extent, that the Earth actually is shaped in this fashion. And if it is hollow, then we no longer need look for the saucers from outer space—but rather from 'inner space!'"

Anyone who had followed the career of Ray Palmer would not have been startled at this assertion. For Palmer had long championed the idea that the earth was hollow, and that its interior contained some sort of supercivilization.

Palmer did not originate the hollow-earth idea; it is quite ancient. But he did give it new life and a new twist with the aid of a fellow by the name of Richard Shaver.

In 1945, when Palmer was editor of the science-fiction magazine *Amazing Stories,* he began publishing a series of "stories" by a Pennsylvania welder named Richard Shaver. Palmer also wrote lengthy editorials about the stories, and there is considerable suspicion that a large part of Shaver's writing was actually done by Palmer, whose style is difficult to hide. In the beginning it was hard to tell whether Palmer was trying to tell the readers that these stories were fictional or true.

The first of the Shaver tales, "I Remember Lemuria," seemed to go down well, and more followed. Palmer got bolder and bolder in proclaiming that these stories were not stories at all, but authentic parts of earth's history brought to light by Richard Shaver's "racial memory."

The general theme of the Shaver stories was that at one time the earth had been populated by a great supercivilization—one that may have come from space. But this civilization was destroyed by a cosmic cataclysm. Some of earth's inhabitants escaped the cataclysm in spaceships, while others retreated underground. There, in huge caverns, they continued their civilization as best they could with the aid of their advanced technology. But underground life caused them to degenerate. One of their technological productions was the Dero or detrimental robot. These creatures had great power, not only underground but on the surface as well, and were responsible for much current human misery.

All of this was presented in a rather confusing fashion and garnished with tales of dashing heroes with ray guns and swords, lush women with "otherworldly" beauty, strange secrets slowly revealed by "the Elder Race," visitors from other planets, narrow escapes, horrible monsters, and all the other elements of cheap science fiction.

It would have been difficult for an outsider to tell that this wasn't standard pulp science fiction. But Palmer began insisting, with increasing stridency, that it wasn't. And people started to believe him. Others began to "remember" the "lost" ages described by Shaver. Some began to blame evil Deros for their misfortunes, and a few even saw the Deros creeping up out of the ground to get them.

When the UFO phenomena caught fire, Palmer more

or less abandoned Shaver's underground world for the more glamorous realms of outer space. By 1959 he was back underground again, but this time claiming that "the flying saucer mystery" and "the Shaver mystery" were connected. Shaver and Palmer later had a falling out, and Shaver insisted that his old editor had given his material "an occult slant" and thus he has been misinterpreted ever since. But Shaver claimed (and, as far as I can determine, continues to claim) that his stories were basically the results of "a realistic research presented through fiction in order to reach as many readers as possible."

Shaver's theories, when boiled down to their basics, sound very much like those of Erich von Däniken, though they are a good ten years older. "Earth was colonized, in the beginning," Shaver wrote, "by water breathing races from space. . . . These space voyagers and their wisdom and language are described in the 'rock books.'"

According to Shaver, virtually every rock surface on earth was inscribed or sculptured in some way by the ancients, and the remains of their work, though scattered and eroded by time and natural processes, is still visible—to those who look hard enough and know what they are looking for.

"For instance, in Tarzan, where he stands before a shot of Victoria Falls, just behind him in the dubbed-in shot, is a tremendous female figure whose head and shoulders project above the falls. Badly battered by time, she is still there, forever bathing in these tremendous cataracts of water. I find this is true of many photos of waterfalls, not only Victoria Falls.

"For instance, just to the right of Gutzen Borglum's

work in the granite, where he carved the huge Lincoln, Jefferson, etc. [the Mount Rushmore monument in South Dakota], there is a much more ancient head showing where some ancient sculptor had the same idea, and this head shows in some of the photos of this sculpture."

But when Ray Palmer said that flying saucers came from "inner space," he was not relying on Richard Shaver's racial memory alone. As I mentioned, the idea that the earth is hollow is far from new. For centuries hell was a very real and tangible place found somewhere under the ground. The "entrance to hell" has been located countless times. Usually it was found in the country of one's enemy.

There were serious and scholarly speculations about huge underground caves. One seventeenth-century scholar said that dragons lived in underground caves, and that is why we saw so few of them. Siberian tribesmen who found the frozen remains of woolly mammoths, assumed that they were the remains of creatures that lived in a subterranean world. The Siberians could not conceive of extinct animals that had lived thousands of years ago, but vast underground worlds came quite naturally to them. According to legend, dwarfs lived in underground caves, and most accounts placed the realm of fairies under the earth as well.

By the seventeenth century there was a full-fledged hollow-earth theory, based on scientific speculation rather than religious or mystical speculation or common folklore. The theory was proposed by Edmund Halley, an astronomer of considerable fame. Halley first calculated the orbit of the comet that now bears his name. Halley thought that the earth's crust was about five miles thick.

Inside this shell was another hollow ball, about the size of the planet Venus. Inside that another, the size of Mars, and finally a solid inner core the size of the planet Mercury.

Moreover, Halley proposed the idea that these inner earth's could be inhabited, and were kept bright by a luminous gas. The Northern Lights, he said, were the result of this gas escaping in the polar region. Halley knew that the poles of the earth were slightly flattened, thus he reasoned the crust would be thinner there, and allow the interior gas to escape more easily.

As knowledge of the structure of our planet increased, hollow-earth theories lost popularity among scientists. But they did not disappear altogether. In early nineteenth century a retired U. S. Army captain named John Cleves Symmes came up with the idea that not only was the earth hollow, but that there were large openings at the poles by which the center of the hollow earth could be reached. The ocean flowed in and out of these polar holes, he said. As far as I have been able to determine, this idea of holes at the poles was original with Symmes, and even if it wasn't, he said it was, and the theoretical holes are now called Symmes' Holes.

Symmes was a true believer. He spent the final years of his life traveling around the country lecturing about his theory, and trying to raise money for an expedition to the North Pole to find the polar hole. He never did get money for the expedition, but he did actually get twenty-five votes in Congress to authorize funds for such a venture. That wasn't enough, and Symmes died in 1829 a frustrated and disappointed man. As a monument to this prophet without honor, his son put up a large stone model of the hollow earth over his grave in Hamilton, Ohio.

Nearly a hundred years later, though Symmes's theories were still in circulation, though they were often uncredited. Marshall B. Gardner, who thought the earth was hollow, said its interior was lighted by a small sun. Gardner ridiculed many of Symmes's ideas as absurd, but he stole the most original of them, the idea that there were large holes at the North and South Pole.

Gardner was still alive, however, when the polar explorer Admiral Richard E. Byrd flew over first the North Pole in 1926 and three years later flew over the South Pole. Gardner had spent a lot of time "proving" that previous polar explorers had simply missed the holes. But Byrd's flights were harder to account for, because according to Gardner, the holes had diameters of fifteen hundred miles. How could Byrd have missed them? Gardner had no explanation and wrote nothing else on the subject of the hollow earth.

But there were others who kept the faith by insisting that Byrd had not missed the holes at all, that he had in fact found them, and the whole story was being "hushed up" for some obscure reason. The rumor that Admiral Byrd's "discovery" is being kept secret by the government has to be one of the most persistent unsupported tales in the history of America. I have been asked about it dozens of times, and when I reply the story is silly, and point to the enormous amount of polar exploration that has taken place over the last few decades, people have refused to believe me. They assume that I too am a dupe of the conspiracy of silence, or actually an active participant in it.

Ray Palmer deserves part of the credit (or blame) for keeping the Byrd discovery story alive. "When (Byrd's) plane took off from its Arctic base," Palmer wrote, "it proceeded straight north to the Pole. From that point it flew a total of 1,700 miles beyond the Pole and then retraced its course to its Arctic base. As progress was made beyond the Pole point, iceless lands and lakes, mountains covered with trees, and even monstrous animals moving through the underbrush, were observed and reported via radio by the plane's occupants . . ." It sounds a bit like the polar land described on the Piri Re'is map.

A little later in the same article Palmer proclaimed, "That land, on today's maps, CANNOT EXIST. But since it DOES, we can only conclude that today's maps are incorrect, incomplete, and do not present a true picture of the northern hemisphere!"

What it came down to, in Palmer's view, was that Byrd had flown a little way into the inner earth. He assumed that far longer flights had been made into the hollow earth since that time but had gone unreported. This became an important part of his argument that flying saucers came from inside the earth.

The tale of what Admiral Byrd was supposed to have seen had a rather simple beginning. In 1929, David E. Bunger, a pilot on the Byrd expedition landed his seaplane at one of the many then unexplored Antarctic coastal areas that is ice-free. He said that it looked like an "oasis" of ice-free lakes and that the water seemed remarkably warm. Palmer added the trees and monstrous animals moving through the underbrush.

What is genuinely intriguing about such stories is

that they never die. This one has been making the rounds of weird and occult-type publications for years, and it popped up once again in Charles Berlitz' enormously successful book, *The Bermuda Triangle*. Berlitz has added "what looked like primitive men" to the scene. It is called a glimpse "through a hole into another dimension."

Palmer had a number of other arguments to support his hollow-earth ideas. The stomachs of frozen mammoths were supposed to contain vegetation that could not possibly have grown in northern climates, thus they must have wandered out of the warmer inner earth and frozen to death. The musk ox, says Palmer, migrates northward in the winter. The implication is that it is heading for its true home inside the earth.

And just in case the hole in the pole theory becomes a little hard to accept, Palmer had another suggestion as to how these UFOs get to the surface from inside of the hollow earth. They come through the earth's crust "the same way a ghost goes through a door." Is that all clear now?

Books on the hollow earth still continue to appear from time to time. Yet it would be incorrect to imply that hollow-earth theories have, or are likely to get, a very large following any more. If anything is certain in this uncertain world, it is that the interior of the earth is not hollow and does not contain any vast super-civilizations. But it is useful to recall just how long these ideas have been around. For someday you might hear a rumor that the government is "covering up" information that there is a great big hole in the pole that leads to the hollow center of the earth. If you are unprepared for such news, it can be quite startling.

A more original idea for the origin of UFOs and a lot of other strange things was proposed by Ivan Sanderson in his 1970 book *Invisible Residents.* Sanderson said that there might be a highly advanced civilization beneath the sea, and that these highly civilized sea beings have developed their own type of "space travel" which takes them into our atmosphere—hence UFOs. Fort had made a similar suggestion but never followed it up.

Sanderson's arguments, while rather complicated, essentially rest on three main points. First, life originally evolved in the sea, therefore these theoretical sea beings would have had much longer to evolve a high intelligence than land-bound man. Second, there is a great deal that we don't know about the sea. Third, an awful lot of strange things happen in or near water. He estimated that the majority of UFO reports concerned things sighted over or near a body of water, and a lot of ships and planes disappear in the ocean.

This theory, while rather interesting, doesn't really hang together. What manner of beings are these underwater creatures? Sanderson didn't even really venture a guess—indeed he did not come out flatly and say that they are material beings at all. He referred to them as "things" or "forces."

Well "things," "forces," or superfish, they certainly don't appear to act in any consistent or logical way. Why should they take the trouble to hide from us on the one hand, and send UFOs skittering all over the place on the other? Why should they make planes or ships disappear? There may be no logic to their actions at all. Sanderson theorizes that they may be "overcivilized and quite mad." Their technology is so incredible that "they could live anywhere or everywhere, and move about instantly, or faster, anywhere throughout space and/or time."

The mention of moving through time brings us to one final theory concerning the origin of UFOs—that they come from some other time or other "dimension." Time travel or creatures from another dimension are both basically science-fiction concepts. Not that they are scientifically "impossible"—whatever that may mean —it is just that we have no evidence one way or the other about the subjects. It's not even an area in which scientists can make educated guesses.

The scientist-writer C. P. Snow once said that in science it was important to know what not to think about. Time travel and other dimensions are things not to think about, primarily because thinking about them, at our present state of knowledge, leads nowhere. But still, speculating on such subjects can be fun and harmless, unless we get carried away with our own theories.

UFOs from the future would clear up a lot of problems. For one thing it would explain why the creatures that are often described as piloting the craft usually look so human. Would creatures from other planets necessarily look like us?

Then it would explain why these visitors are so interested in what we are doing that they keep coming back. We might be of great interest to our descendants, but would we be interesting enough to strangers for them to repeatedly travel light years to check up on how we were getting along?

Then there is the business of predictions. Historically and in more recent UFO cases, the aliens often issue prophecies about what is going to happen. How would

175

they know the future?—unless, of course, they had been there.

Why do UFOs historical and current appear to pop in and pop out of our view—with obvious disregard for the laws of physics? They have already overcome time, why not space? It would also account for the reason why UFOs are not tracked successfully by the various radar networks—we possess the technology to track objects through space, but not through time. And all these disappearances, people, planes, ships, why is no trace ever found? Because they drop right through the hole in time. They are gone without a trace.

There are of course special problems with this interpretation. Can the future alter the past? In practical terms, what would happen if a man from the future came back and kidnaped his own ancestor?

One could, I suppose, continue this sort of fantasy for some time. Such speculations have already served as the basis for countless science-fiction tales. That is the realm for which they are best suited.

12

THE GREAT SECRETS

We are now going to look at the ancient-astronauts theory in terms of the occult tradition. Now you might object that this isn't proper. We are dealing with a scientific and historical inquiry. Why introduce occultism, or any other sort of "mystic nonsense?"

But I did not invent the relationship. A large percentage of the writings on this subject are frankly occult in nature. Even those books which are not avowedly occult often rely heavily on occult material.

Besides, occultism isn't a dirty word. The word simply means secret or hidden. Occult tradition holds that there exists in the world a body of important knowledge that is unknown to the population at large. This knowledge may have been "lost" because civilizations were destroyed along with their books and documents. This knowledge may also be deliberately kept hidden from the general public. The purpose for hiding the information may be evil, a conspiracy of silence. One of the most frequently mentioned conspiracies in occult circles is a reputed conspiracy among the world's religious leaders to suppress or mistranslate portions of the Bible. The most frequently mentioned reason for such a conspiracy, is that if "the truth" were known, organized religion would crumble. Occultists are generally pretty suspicious of organized religion anyway. Organized religion returns the compliment.

Hiding knowledge is not necessarily evil. Great Secrets may be kept because the world is "not ready" to receive them. Great Secrets of this kind are generally supposed to be passed down through the ages by a small but powerful group of adepts, or initiates, in secret societies. The secrets are revealed only to those who are deemed worthy, and often the very existence of such a group is itself a secret—though such adepts may in fact control the world. Secretly, of course.

How does an individual outside of the charmed circle ever find out about these secrets in the first place? One way is to come across an ancient book or scroll— thought to have been lost for centuries—which reveals part of the story.

The famed Dead Sea Scrolls, found unexpectedly in a cave near the Dead Sea, are an excellent example of such an unexpected discovery. Occultists are often pointing to the discovery of the Dead Sea Scrolls, as an indication of how "lost" knowledge can be rediscovered.

Even Erich von Däniken, who is not avowedly an occultist, has claimed a discovery of this sort. He starts his book *The Gold of the Gods*, with a description of his visit to a cave in Ecuador, in which he was shown a "metal library" of incredible antiquity, and written in an unknown language.

He asks: "Is it [our age] prepared to decipher an age-old work even if it means bringing to light truths that might turn our neat but dubious world picture completely upside down?

"Do not the high priests of all religions ultimately abhor revelations about prehistory that might replace *belief* in the creation by *knowledge* of the creation."

There are some problems with Von Däniken s discovery, however. The man who he says took him into the cave denies that he ever did so, and the Ecuadorian authorities who claim to have been in the cave say it contains nothing but birds. Where this leaves the metallic library is anybody's guess. But it is one point, and only one of many, at which the subject of ETIs and occult tradition touch. Books on the subject of ETIs are often filled with references to secret or hidden documents.

Another way of discovering occult secrets is to meet one or several of the "adepts" or members of a secret society that know the Great Secrets and have him reveal them. The French author Robert Charroux is one of the most prolific and popular authors on ETI themes. He claims not only are the Great Secrets of the ancients in the care of certain secret societies, but that some of the adepts have helped him compose his books. In the foreword to one of Charroux books, *The Gods Unknown,* André Bouguenec writes, "Robert Charroux is not the sole author of this book. True, he has written it, he has carried out the research, selected and planned the material, laid the foundations, argued his points. He had scoured the archives of the world in search of original and unpublished documents. But he has had a great many collaborators.

"Some of these fellow-workers are very far out of the ordinary. He has been instructed by Exalted Beings, some of whom may be the unknown Masters of the World. They have taught him little by little, one thing

179

at a time, disclosing their secrets as it were on a predetermined plan."

Charroux's collaborators have strange names, like Master of Angles and the High Priest Anubis Schenouda, "an Egyptian initiate." There are also "certain authentic Druids, such as the mysterious Mn. Y." and someone called Gregori B., "who has re-established the Inca Religion of the Sun." And above them all is the Maha, the master of masters and head of the Unknown Superiors. Bouguenec says that the Unknown Masters have read Charroux's work with approval and "answers are suggested if not actually given."

This process of disclosing information little by little or suggesting rather than giving answers is common to all occult writing, and common to much that has been written about ETIs. It also creates tremendous problems for the non-occultist. At any given moment all he may have is a mass of unconnected and unsupported and often contradictory statements. Reading occult material can be frustrating, for you have the feeling that you are never being given the full story, and the suspicion grows that there is no full story. But just wait, say the confirmed occultists, "the truth" will be revealed in due time, and that time is near.

One always seems to be moving toward a goal that can never be reached. Behind one "master" or "high council" stands another, even more masterful or higher. There are more revelations, often reversing the previous revelations. But about it all hangs an air of hopeful expectancy and exciting mystery. For some this apparently never-ending series of revelations from on high holds great fascination.

There is also what might be called direct revelation. In

this case there are no dusty documents or secret meetings with Unknown Masters—the information is received telepathically or psychically. The information may be coming from the ETIs who communicate with the UFO contactees, or the gods, or the semi-divine masters, or it may be coming from someplace else.

Occultists often speak of "the akashic records," a collection containing everything that has happened or ever will happen in the universe. These records aren't written down, or stored on microfilm or anything else, they are just there. Certain individuals with special powers are believed to be able to tap the akashic records and thus produce prophecies about the future or tell us about lost civilizations of the past or life on planets of other galaxies.

The extremely popular American seer Edgar Cayce claimed to be psychically in touch with the akashic records. Aside from predicting the future, Cayce also had a great deal to say about the past. Though he never spoke specifically of ETIs, his statements are couched in the vague and tortured language apparently preferred by prophets, so one can imply ETIs.

Cayce's statements, particularly about Atlantis, are often mentioned by ETI theorists. Atlantis, according to some theories, was founded by the ETIs.

In the book *Gods and Spacemen in the Ancient West,* which is billed as "The ultimate proof of super-beings from space!" author W. Raymond Drake says: "A gifted Seer may obtain accurate information by methods unknown to science. Edgar Cayce in Reading 378–16 revealed that a record of Atlantis from its beginnings to final destruction will be found in an underground chamber between the paws of the Sphinx."

Then there is the theory of the Cosmic Mind. According to this theory (or theories for there are many variations) all human consciousness, perhaps all intelligent consciousness in the universe, and perhaps even all living things including plants are somehow interconnected in a great universal web of consciousness, but most of us are unaware of this. It is hinted that the true "Master of Masters" is in fact this Universal or Cosmic Mind, and that the mission of the ETIs is to prepare the human race for recognition or awakening to this ultimate fact.

By now, though, we are pretty far out, and before we lose our way entirely, let us return to earth for a while to try to discover how this whole idea of occult knowledge got started, and what relationship it might have to ETI visits in the distant past.

There is a very definite, and very ancient, feeling in the West at least, that things were much better a long time ago and we have been sliding downhill ever since. As far as we can determine, this tradition of "the good old days" started in Mesopotamia, among the earliest known civilizations. It was expressed by the ancient Hebrews, who were much influenced by the Mesopotamian civilizations, in the idea of the Fall of Man, and the feeling that the people of the days of the Patriarchs were a nobler breed. The Book of Genesis informs us in some detail how the early descendants of Adam lived many hundreds of years.

Christianity picked up the mood, and placed even more emphasis on the concept of the Fall of Man. Throughout Christian history there has been a constant harkening back to the Age of the Apostles, or some other long past time. Within the first few centuries after Christ, a lot of Christians began to believe that while miracles had been common once, the days of miracles were over.

The Greeks and Romans had their own traditions of a Lost Golden Age. And in addition they had a variety of mystery religions and secret societies. In both the mystery religions and the secret societies, an individual generally had to go through a long and difficult period of training and testing before he (or she, for some of the mysteries were open only to women) were given the "secrets" possessed by the group. The process of learning the secrets was one of slowly unfolding knowledge, as the initiate moved up in the hierarchy of the group. This knowledge was usually supposed to be incredibly ancient.

A blending of Christian and occult traditions can be found in the movement called *gnosticism*. The word *gnosos* is Greek for knowledge, and the gnostics taught that they, and they alone, possessed a "secret" knowledge, about God and the universe.

Orthodox Christians regarded gnostics as heretics but also often feared them as powerful magicians, individuals who possessed real power based upon their secret knowledge. Gnosticism was extremely influential during the early years of the Christian era, until it was finally overwhelmed by orthodox Christianity. But various religious groups claiming to possess secret knowledge have continued to crop up throughout history. And even today there are a number of religious groups claiming to possess the secret knowledge of the ancient gnostics.

The medieval alchemists, who were trying, among other things to turn lead to gold, and discover the "water of immortality," were also seekers after hidden knowledge. They did not contend that they were trying to discover any new process, but rather that they were attempting to rediscover a very ancient one, for it was generally believed that in ancient times some people had known how to turn lead into gold, but that the information had been lost or hidden. One of the most famous and reputedly most successful of all alchemists was the fourteenth-century Frenchman Nicolas Flamel. Flamel had reputedly discovered the secret of turning base metals into gold after finding an old book attributed to Abraham.

The alchemist Nicolas Flamel.

A huge variety of secret societies claiming occult knowledge flourished throughout Europe from the end of the Middle Ages right to the present day. In the past, such occult societies have attributed their secrets to the Egyptians, the Magi, the "hidden teachings" of Jesus, the refugees from Atlantis, the Tibetans, the ancient Mayans, and a host of other sources. Today, they are increasingly turning to ETIs as the source of their secrets. But to the outsider at least, all of this looks very much like the same old occultism dressed up in a slightly new costume.

In his book *One Hundred Thousand Years of Man's Unknown History,* Robert Charroux presents the new brand of occultism in its purist form. He theorizes (or has had revealed to him) that uncounted millennia ago, ETIs visited earth and transmitted to the human race some of the advanced technology that they possessed. Charroux even dedicates his book to "The first man who, in the distant past, came to Earth from another planet . . ."

The result of this contact between the human race and the ETIs were the great civilizations created by our Superior Ancestors. Then at some point in the distant past there was a great catastrophe, that destroyed all of the great civilizations. Not only were the scientific and/or magical secrets of the Superior Ancestors lost, but all trace and memory of them disappeared as well. However, the disappearance was not complete. A few select survivors preserved the knowledge. They held it in secret because the human race had relapsed into barbarism, and was therefore no longer capable of handling the power of the secrets conveyed.

Charroux toys with the idea that the catastrophe was an ancient thermonuclear war, and because of the destruction that the human race brought down upon itself through the technology given to it by the ETIs, it was decided that we were no longer worthy of the knowledge. (The idea of an ancient thermonuclear war is one that crops up frequently in this area.) So it was decided (by whom is not clear) that the Great Secrets would be hidden from the common run of humanity. He sees secrecy as playing a major role in human history.

"Even today, only the highest dignitaries initiates of Freemasonry, for example, know its plans for social evolution. The same is true of the Catholic Church. The popes, or at least those of them who have been initiates, have always kept secrets without betraying them. It is even possible that they have had advance knowledge of great historical occurrences such as wars, persecutions and social upheavals, without trying to oppose the natural course of events.

"The secrets . . . were transmitted by co-optation, to initiates regarded as particularly worthy. These men were almost certainly religious leaders. The Book of the Great Secrets was probably recopied and rectified several times throughout the centuries. Precepts drawn from it have served as the basis of all the great religions . . ."

Among the initiates who Charroux believes were party to the Great Secrets were Moses, Pythagoras, Plato, and Jesus. "It is amazing to think," he writes, "that for more than two hundred generations men were given the mission of confiding to other men fantastic revelations which were not to be made public, and not one of them ever

186

cried out, 'I know the Great Secrets and I'm going to reveal them!'"

All this is fairly standard occult lore; the only difference is that Charroux credits the ETIs with the origin of the Great Secrets. He even hints that the Rosicrucians may be the bearers of the Great Secrets. The Rosicrucians was a secret society that first announced its existence in Germany about 400 years ago. The members claimed to possess all sorts of magical knowledge, like the formula for changing lead into gold. It was also said that the tomb of their founder was illuminated by a light that burned forever. This is the sort of tale which makes seekers of ancient technology sit up and take notice.

You have almost certainly seen advertisements from the Rosicrucian Society (AMORC) which promise that if you fill out the attached coupon and mail it to Scribe XYZ, you too can become initiate and learn the "Secrets Entrusted to a Few." Actually the mail-order Rosicrucians AMORC, or Ancient and Mystical Order Rosae Crucis, isn't very ancient. It was begun in the early twentieth century by a New York advertising man with an interest in occultism.

In fact, there is no hard historical evidence that there ever was a real Rosicrucian Society at all. There is considerable suspicion that the whole thing was started as an elaborate joke by a group of German students in the sixteenth century. But Charroux says that there are, "real Rosicrucians," and that they may be the bearers of the Great Secrets.

The Australian writer Andrew Tomas dedicates his popular ETI book *We Are Not the First* to "the Comte de Saint-Germain, who in the words of Voltaire, 'never dies and knows everything.'" Voltaire had a great sense of humor, and he was surely joking when he referred to St. Germain in those words. St. Germain was something of a man of mystery in the mid eighteenth century. No one knows who he really was, though there were many rumors. He was credited with possessing all sorts of marvelous secrets, including the secret of eternal life. St. Germain never exactly claimed that he could do all of these things people said he could, but he never denied that he could either. He just went about acting mysterious and letting people believe whatever they wanted about him. A few did regard him as a wonder worker, though most thought of him as an elegant and charming faker. But he has been a popular occult figure for two centuries, and countless occult societies have been formed in his name. The Comte de Cagliostro, who is better known today, was St. Germain's younger contemporary and imitator. He was a good deal less successful, for while Cagliostro died in prison, St. Germain died at an advanced age in the home of a wealthy patron. And there are always those, of course, who say that he never died.

Tomas credits St. Germain with space flights to the outer planets and time travel. He ends his tribute to the occultist with these words:

"Transmutation, extension of life, space travel, time conquest—all are frontiers of science. It can be surmised that the Comte de Saint-Germain had access to the secret fountain of knowledge."

Louis Pauwels and Jacques Bergier postulate all manner of secret societies in their occult bestseller *The Morning of the Magicians.* One of their more startling ideas is a secret society of superintelligent mutants operating in the world today:

"Intelligent and rational mutants, endowed with an infallible memory, and a constantly lucid intelligence are perhaps working beside us disguised as country schoolmasters or insurance agents.

"Do these mutants form an invisible society? No human being lives alone. He can only develop himself with a society. The human society we know has shown only too well its hostility towards an objective intelligence or a free imagination . . . If there are mutants answering to our description, there is every reason to believe that they are working and communicating with one another in a society superimposed on our own, which no doubt extends all over the world . . ."

There is in most occult speculation a touch of paranoia, a conspiracy that someone or something is out to get them, or in the very least to make sure that their truths are never heard. Such a feeling runs strongly in the works of most ETI theorists as well. If they do not

St. Germain.

claim there is an actual conspiracy on the part of orthodox science against them, they say that the gross stupidity and stubbornness of most scientists amounts to a conspiracy.

It is impossible for them to believe that the truths, which seem so painfully obvious, can remain unseen by others. The answer must be incredible stupidity or conspiracy, and of the two conspiracy appears to make more sense.

One popular book on the ETI theme was dedicated by its author to "our publishers for having the guts to publish it." Though the sentiment was doubtless genuine, the book had an excellent sale, and "the guts" were amply rewarded.

In the past those who believed, or at least said that they possessed occult knowledge, often tried to form their own secret societies, or their own religions. The boundary between a secret society and a religion tends to become a bit hazy. Ancient astronaut lore has already been incorporated by some occult groups, and a whole new branch of occultism may be forming around it. There are already a few "ancient astronaut societies" and there has been at least one convention of ancient astronaut "seekers" that I know of.

Von Däniken is outspokenly unreligious, even anti-religious. At the close of his book *The Gold of the Gods,* he launches a furious diatribe against all religions. "I am convinced that religions with their countless gods hinder progress. How often have religions and sects, each of them vowed to one god, been the cause of wars, misery and abominations! And if their insight does not improve, they will be a contributing cause to the end of human existence."

And yet he also suggests that we are all part of a great cosmic IT, which he calls a "synonym for the concept GOD." To support his argument he quotes from the Book of Revelation in the Bible. For he says that St. John the Divine must have had access to "secret texts" in which the origin of all being was described:

"In the beginning was the Word, and the Word was with God, and the Word was God.

"All things were made by him; and without him was not anything made that was made."

This IT, says Von Däniken, existed before the Big Bang which created our universe. We are all part of that IT, blown apart in the Big Bang. But the explosion did not result in a chaotic universe, for all of the bits of the IT, that is us and all of the other consciousness in the universe, have been programmed to come together again at some time in the future. Only then will the meaning of it all come clear to us. The idea is not original. It is quite similar to the beliefs expressed by the Essenes, an ancient Jewish sect and the Gnostics, an early heretical Christian group.

How did Von Däniken learn all of this? It is pure speculation, he admits, and perhaps a bit more than speculation, for he quotes with obvious approval this statement from theologian Robert Pucetti, "Knowledge does not necessarily have to be won on scientific paths and in fact no so-called religious truth of importance has ever been arrived at in this way." Thus, Erich von Däniken, the leading spokesman for "scientific" explanation of religious myths appears to be leaving the door to mystic revelation wide open.

Richard R. Lingeman, an editor of the New York

Times Book Review must have gotten somewhat the same sort of feeling after an interview with Von Däniken, for he wrote:

"One half expects—hysterical vision of my own—von Däniken's next book announcing that he has at last been taken up some obscure mount and shown a genuine ancient astronauts' time capsule, with laser beam-inscribed tables bearing detailed instructions to mankind. The thought of a new astro-religion, with Erich von Däniken as its prophet gives one pause."

13

CLOSING ARGUMENTS

From astronomy to occultism is a long journey. But as we said in the very first chapter, a huge array of subjects enters into the discussion of ETI contact. I have tried to give a representative sample of the arguments for and against. Now it's time to offer some opinions.

The ETI theorists themselves admit that their ideas are unusual, even bizarre. Certainly the theory that in ancient times highly advanced extraterrestrials visited the earth and gave to the human race much of the knowledge that makes us uniquely human is not the sort of information that one is going to find in an average history book. Such a theory is, in terms of conventional scholarship and science, wildly improbable. It is the duty of the supporter of the improbable to prove that it happened; it is not the duty of his opponents to prove that the improbable didn't happen. It is very difficult to prove a negative anyway.

On this basis I must conclude that the case for ETI contact is unproven—not that I know for certain that it didn't happen, certainly not because I can prove that it couldn't happen. It is simply that there is not enough convincing evidence that it did happen.

I don't believe that I started out with any undue prejudices against intelligent life elsewhere in the universe. It is difficult for me to see how we could be unique.

I also don't believe that I have any great emotional resistance to the idea of our having been visited by creatures of superior intellect. If such were proved to be the case I suppose that I might find the idea a bit upsetting. But my opinion of the human race is not such an exalted one that evidence proving we were not the apex of nature would shatter me. Quite to the contrary. I think that the knowledge that superior intelligences were out there somewhere in their spaceships watching over us would be comforting. We seem to be making such a mess of things on our own, it would be nice to believe that the ETIs could swoop down and save us, before we destroy ourselves entirely. It is certainly more ennobling to think of ourselves as children of the stars than as the naked ape.

But just because the thought is a nice one does not make it so. We need evidence, and because the theory is so improbable we need lots of it. Clear and convincing evidence is what we lack.

There is a difference between evidence and mysteries, which is not always obvious in the argument of those who believe in extraterrestrial contact. I cannot explain with any certainty what happened in Siberia in June 1908. I do not know for sure how the Egyptians constructed the Great Pyramid, or why the people of the Nazca Desert made huge drawings in the earth. I don't know what Ezekiel saw, or what happened to the five planes that disappeared in 1945 in the Bermuda Triangle. I cannot tell you who Kaspar Hauser was, and

I cannot produce the corpse of Cagliostro. So there are a lot of unexplained things in the world.

The theory of extraterrestrial contact provides us with answers of a sort for all of these mysteries and many many more. But the method by which these answers are provided is just too easy.

The theory holds that the ETIs are so unimaginably advanced that they can do absolutely anything. They can overcome the distances between the stars, perhaps even time itself. Yet their minds are utterly alien to us so what they do doesn't have to make any sense—they can issue prophecies to Ezekiel and steal airplanes out of the sky. Since the ETIs don't have to conform to any rules at all, they can be trotted out as a solution to all mysteries. Again, I must stress, I am not trying to prove that such things couldn't happen, or didn't happen, merely that there is no particular reason to believe that they did happen.

The archaeological and historical evidence cited for ETIs—the monuments, the myths, and the rest—are all capable of a variety of interpretations. We have looked at some of the different interpretations this evidence has been given in the past. Many writers on the subject of ETIs have not been terribly careful about the quality of the evidence that they use to support their theories either. The frequently mentioned *Book of Dyzan* probably does not exist (again it is extremely difficult to prove a negative) and the evidence is not much better to support the existence of the Tully papyrus.

There is also the strong tendency on the part of believers in the ETI hypothesis to both underestimate and overestimate our ancestors. Why is it that we find it so hard to believe that technologically primitive people could have built the Great Pyramid or some of the massive monuments of South America? Peoples whose tools and technology were not a great deal more advanced built the roads and aqueducts of Rome and the cathedrals of medieval Europe. No one, as far as I know, has suggested that the builders of the Appian Way or the Cathedral at Chartres were aided by extraterrestrial technology. The records from Rome and medieval Europe are reasonably good—so we know how they did it. The records from more ancient times, or from cultures like the South American Indians, are far less complete. But just because we don't have the information does not give us leave to assume anything we wish about such peoples.

In overestimating the accomplishments of our ancestors we are simply falling prey to the persistent myths of the "good old days." By making the Great Pyramid some sort of mystic monument to space we may be ignoring the less attractive explanation that it is a monument to a despot, built with years of grinding toil by anonymous masses who lived and died like beasts of burden.

The evidence for the existence of UFOs in the present also suffers from the problem of inconclusiveness. I cannot explain everything that people have been seeing in the sky for the last thirty years, or indeed all the unexplained sightings for thousands of years. But on the basis of the evidence presented thus far I am not willing to accept the explanation that these unexplained sightings are really spaceships.

I guess what I am really waiting for is for the spaceship to land on the White House lawn and for the little green men (or whatever) to step out and present their credentials. Failing that, I might settle for a low-level sweep over a major city witnessed by thousands and confirmed by good, clear motion-picture films, preferably from several sources.

If the ETIs not only contacted us in the past but are continuing in some obscure way to observe us and perhaps even guide us, that is a piece of information that will not only change the way we think but the way we live. It will be the most important discovery in all human history. Before I make any major changes I'm going to require really good evidence, far better than has been presented so far.

The argument of "unproven" isn't a very thrilling one. It's much more fun to think about all those space-

Visitors from space have been a common theme of science fiction. This is one from the film The Day the Earth Stood Still.

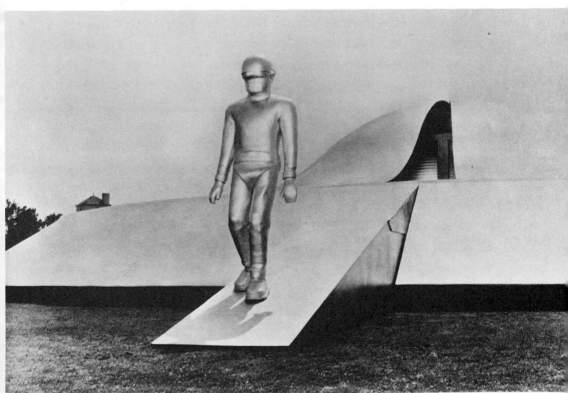

ships landing in the Tigris and Euphrates Valley ten thousand years ago. But we can't assume something is true simply because it is more exciting.

We must also guard against the desire to find patterns where none really exist. The human mind tends to reject the random, the unplanned, or the unexplained. We like to fit it all into one great scheme, which embraces past, present, and future, and "makes sense of it all." But often the real world makes no sense at all, at least none that we can discern within the limits of our information and intellectual abilities.

In reviewing the subject of pyramidology and particularly the work of Charles Piazzi Smyth, the most diligent and brilliant of the pyramidologists, science writer Martin Gardner made some points which are worth remembering when considering the work of the supporters of the extraterrestrial contact hypothesis as well:

"As worthless as all this literature is, it is not entirely worthless if we can see in it an important object lesson. No book has ever demonstrated more clearly than Smyth's (the other Pyramid books, of course, to a lesser degree) how easy it is to work over an undigested mass of data and emerge with a pattern, which at first glance, is so intricately put together that it is difficult to believe it is nothing more than the product of a man's brain. In a sense, this is true of almost all the books of pseudo-scientists. In one way or another, they do not let the data speak for themselves. Consciously or unconsciously, their preconceived dogmas twist and mold the objective facts into forms which support the dogmas, but have no basis in the exterior world. Sir Flinders Petrie, a famous archaeologist who made some highly exact Pyramid measurements, reports that he once caught a Pyramidologist secretly filing down a projecting stone to make it conform to one of his theories!"

The ETI theorists have, it seems to me, twisted and ignored some data, and even on occasion tried the equivalent of filing down an offending stone to make it conform to one of their theories.

There is also a genuinely unpleasant feature to be found in the writings of Von Däniken, Charroux, Sanderson, and the rest. Such writers glory in their "amateur" status, this they say frees them from being "trapped" by the "dogmas" of any particular speciality. With the "freedom" that being amateurs gives them they feel compelled to denounce trained scientists and scholars as blind fools and worse, for failing or refusing to accept their "amateur" theories. Charles Fort was quite outspoken in his scorn for conventional science, later writers are not quite so outspoken, but no less scornful.

It is quite true that scientists and scholars, like the rest of us, can and do become attached to a particular set of ideas. They can even become ferociously dogmatic. But they can also change their minds. There are many examples in the history of science where a well-established theory was overturned in a very short time, in the face of new evidence. It is the evidence that supports a theory which is most important. The less conventional the theory, that is, the larger the number of previously held ideas it seeks to overturn, the better the evidence must be. Sometimes unconventional theories have turned out to be correct, but more often than not they turn out to be wrong! An awful lot of wild theories are floated every year. The vast majority of them have slipped into a well-deserved obscurity. Unexciting as it may be, the conventional explanation has usually turned out to be the right one.

Science is supposed to be a self-correcting system, in which error and dogma are purged in the arena of hard evidence. The system doesn't always work as it is supposed to—indefensible ideas have been defended, and startling new ones rejected almost out of hand. But given the limitations of being a human system, it works pretty well. Most ideas eventually get a fair hearing. Science isn't a monolithic establishment either. There are plenty of angry disagreements within the ranks.

ETI theorists are often fond of comparing themselves to Galileo, who was persecuted for his ideas about the solar system. Galileo's opponents, they point out, even refused to look through the telescope to test the truth of his theories. The analogy, however, doesn't work. Galileo was, in effect, imprisoned for his ideas, and many of his works were banned. No one has been imprisoned, or exiled for saying that extraterrestrials visited the earth. The books, far from being banned, sell in the millions of copies. ETI theorists may not have been invited to publish their ideas in the prestigious scientific journals, or asked to address symposiums—but that hardly qualifies anyone for the Galileo Galilei award for scientific martyrdom.

Unless one wishes to indulge in some of the more elaborate theories of conspiracy, there can be no question of suppression of information. The theories of extraterrestrial contact are out in front of the public, and we can make our own judgments upon them. I have made mine—though I certainly hope and believe that I possess the flexibility of mind to change. It would be hard to remain skeptical if that jet plane was found in an ancient tomb or if a spaceship really did land on the White House lawn.

And you—I trust—will make your own judgments as well.

BIBLIOGRAPHY

Berlitz, Charles. *Mysteries from Forgotten Worlds.* New York: Doubleday, 1972.

Bernard, Raymond. *The Hollow Earth.* New York: University Books, 1969.

Binder, Otto. *Unsolved Mysteries of the Past.* New York: Tower, 1968.

Blumrich, Josef F. *The Spaceships of Ezekiel.* New York: Bantam, 1974.

Charroux, Robert. *Forgotten Worlds.* New York: Walker, 1973.

———. *The Gods Unknown.* New York: Berkley, 1974.

———. *One Hundred Thousand Years of Man's Unknown History.* New York: Berkley, 1971.

Cohen, Daniel. *Myths of the Space Age.* New York: Dodd, Mead, 1967.

———. *Voodoo, Devils and the New Invisible World.* New York: Dodd, Mead, 1972.

Condon, Edward U., and others. *Scientific Study of Unidentified Flying Objects.* New York: Bantam, 1968.

De Camp, L. Sprague. *The Ancient Engineers.* New York: Doubleday, 1973.

Dempewolff, Richard (ed.). *Lost Cities and Forgotten Tribes.* New York, Hearst, 1974.

Dione, R. I. *God Drives a Flying Saucer.* New York: Bantam, 1973.

Downing, Barry H. *The Bible and Flying Saucers.* Philadelphia: Lippincott, 1968.

Drake, W. Raymond. *Gods and Spacemen in the Ancient East.* New York: Signet, 1973.

———. *Gods and Spacemen in the Ancient West.* New York: Signet, 1974.

Flammonde, Paris. *The Age of Flying Saucers.* New York: Hawthorn, 1971.

Flindt, Max H., and Binder, Otto O. *Mankind—Child of the Stars.* New York: Fawcett, 1974.

Fort, Charles. *The Books of Charles Fort.* New York: Henry Holt, 1941.

Gardner, Martin. *Fads and Fallacies in the Name of Science.* New York: Dover, 1957.

Garvin, Richard. *The Crystal Skull.* New York: Doubleday, 1973.

Hapgood, Charles H. *Maps of the Ancient Sea Kings.* Philadelphia: Chilton, 1963.

Holiday. F. W. *Creatures from the Inner Sphere.* New York: Norton, 1973.

BIBLIOGRAPHY

Keel, John A. *Our Haunted Planet*. New York: Fawcett, 1971.

———. *Strange Creatures from Time and Space*. New York: Fawcett, 1970.

———. *UFOs Operation Trojan Horse*. New York: Putnam's, 1970.

Knight, Damon. *Charles Fort, Prophet of the Unexplained*. New York: Doubleday, 1970.

Lore, Gordon I. R., and Deneault, Harold H. *Mysteries of the Skies*. Englewood Cliffs, N.J.: Prentice-Hall, 1968.

Michell, John. *The View Over Atlantis*. New York: Ballantine, 1972.

Pauwels, Louis, and Bergier, Jacques. *The Morning of the Magicians*. New York: Avon, 1968.

Ronan, Colin. *Lost Discoveries*. New York: McGraw-Hill, 1973.

Sagen, Carl, and Shklovsky, I. S. *Intelligent Life in the Universe*. San Francisco: Holden and Day, 1966.

Sanderson, Ivan. *Investigating the Unexplained*. Englewood Cliffs, N.J.: Prentice-Hall, 1972.

———. *Invisible Residents*. New York: World, 1970.

———. *Uninvited Visitors*. New York: Cowles, 1967.

Sullivan, Walter. *We Are Not Alone*. New York: McGraw-Hill, 1966.

Tomas, Andrew. *We Are Not the First*. New York: Putnam's, 1971.

Tompkins, Peter. *Secrets of the Great Pyramid*. New York: Harper and Row, 1971.

BIBLIOGRAPHY

Von Däniken, Erich. *Chariots of the Gods?* New York: Putnam's, 1970.

———. *Gods from Outer Space.* New York: Putnam's, 1971.

———. *The Gold of the Gods.* New York: Putnam's, 1973.

———. *In Search of Ancient Gods.* New York: Putnam's, 1974.

INDEX

DANIEL COHEN is a prolific free-lance writer with more than thirty books for adults and young people in print. Formerly managing editor of *Science Digest* magazine, he has also written extensively on the occult, the supernatural, and the bizarre. Among his books are A NATURAL HISTORY OF UNNATURAL THINGS, IN SEARCH OF GHOSTS, MAGICIANS, WIZARDS AND SORCERERS, and MONSTERS, GIANTS AND LITTLE MEN FROM MARS. His articles have appeared in such magazines as *The Nation, Coronet,* and *Pageant.* Mr. Cohen and his wife, a writer of romantic fiction, and their daughter share a house in Port Jervis, New York, with a large collection of cats and dogs.